PATRINA GOREE

Copyright © 2020 PATRINA GOREE

Book cover and logo design by PATRINA GOREE

Photography acknowledged and by PATRINA GOREE

All rights reserved. It is not legal to reproduce, duplicate, or transmit any part of this document in either electronic means or printed format. Recording of this publication is strictly prohibited. Scanning, copying, and distribution without the author's consent is theft. For permission requests, write to the publisher addressed.

Any references and stories told in this text are real situations according to the author's life. All names, if used, in this book are with positive image. All photos in this book are acknowledged or were taken by the author.

ISBN: 978-0-578-70974-1 (Paperback)

Library of Congress Control Number (LCCN): 2020910900

Publisher Details:

PATRINA GOREE
PDG Family Holdings, LLC
www.toolsbeyondsports.com

This book is dedicated to:

* Jack Yates, my high school. The coaches and athletes that have represented and will represent while giving their best. These are my roots and where I began to face my journey. Yates is the place where my growth started as an athlete and as a person.
* Every athlete. I am a fan of you. We are one of the unique groups of people on Earth, never forget that! I hope that this book will inspire you to keep being your best so that you can continue to walk in your greatness when you retire.
* Anyone who is reading this book. You have it for a reason, and I hope that this book allows you to see yourself at your most vulnerable and resilient state.
* My journey through sports. Without it, I wouldn't be able to share my truth through this book that I created.
* My family, friends, coaches, and the game of basketball!

TABLE OF CONTENTS

INTRODUCTION

    THE ANCHOR 3

    IDENTITY HUNT 43

    PRE-SEASON CONDITIONING 59

    RESPECT THE GAME 73

    CREATE A TEAM 83

    GET IN THE GAME 91

    GET ON OFFENSE 111

    DEVELOP OTHER SKILLS 117

    MOVE WITH A PURPOSE 123

    CREATE A PLAY 131

    CONTROL THE FLOW AND TEMPO 141

    WINS AND LOSSES 147

OVERTIME 153

Bibliography 155

Acknowledgments 157

About the Author 159

INTRODUCTION

T.O.O.L's Beyond Sports (Taking Ownership of Our Lives Beyond Sports) is designed to help athletes transition in life after sports. While sports build character traits and teach principles, many athletes lose their identity when transitioning. The struggle to find their purpose, beyond sports, is real. Whether in pursuit of their current playing days or when they are at the end of their athletic journey, all athletes must accept a transition from their sport one day. As athletes, we are a unique group of people in this world, and we are already put in positions to adapt and make adjustments more often than anyone else. Life is not about what happens to us but rather how we respond to all things that happen in our lives.

The purpose of this book is to help athletes realize that they already have the tools to transition in life after sports. They have the necessary tools, indicating that life does not have to end when our playing days end. While on our journey, it's hard to focus on life after sports because we have a different focus while in the moments of enjoying the game we play. The tools discussed in each chapter were topics that I chose because they made the most sense and helped me realize the bigger picture of my life, near the end of my athletic career. My goal is to be as clear and relatable to help you as well.

To be honest, life after sports shouldn't be your primary focus if you are currently playing. I expect that it is your primary focus to give your sport everything that you have, with gratitude, if you're still involved. One problem that I noticed is that many of us become stagnant because we don't take ownership of our lives beyond sports. We do not realize that we have the tools to transition in life, and the past becomes a blur.

This book is not a "how-to" or "quick scheme" book that will give you a step by step guide of how to transition beyond sports. It is already inside of you. As athletes, we know that excellent results are only a product of putting in the work. It starts with self. You have to take ownership of your life. When it's time to transition, we should be celebrating, believing, and knowing that, "I gave the game everything that I had, no matter what comes next in my life."

For those of you who are still playing, keep growing as an athlete and as a person. Growth should never end. For those near the end, transitioning, or retiring, embrace the changes that are happening and keep growing as well. It's okay to dream again. Always remember your foundation and why you do the things that you do. Life is real. Be creative in your approach.

You have spent a lot of time preparing to reach the level that you are already on. You knew what you wanted, and you went after it. Your head is already in the game. You currently have an excellent support ecosystem of all of the people you have met this far. Remember all of the sacrifices that you've made to get where you are today? There was purpose in your moves. Wins and losses come with the game, but don't get stagnant, create a play! LET'S GO! To all current, former, and future athletes: I SEE YOU, I AM YOU & I GOT YOU!

Although this book is for athletes, these tools can be a resource for all. Two critical constants in life: CHANGE AND TIME. Who we are is more important than what we do. We cannot buy or replace time.

1st Quarter

Set the Tone

THE ANCHOR
"Foundation & Why"

1

"Most people want to skip the process, not knowing that when you skip steps, you miss the lessons. If you start small and build on what you have, you can continue to multiply that into something greater, while picking up all of the valuable lessons along the way. You learn all of the secrets to the game on your way up. If you're not willing to embrace getting it off of the curb, you're going to fumble anyway once you get your hands on something substantial."

-NIPSEY HUSSLE

(Mitchell, 2018).

I wanted to start this book with a foundation, so this first chapter is about THE ANCHOR. The foundation is the root of anything of significance. My purpose is to share my experiences and these tools with you at this present moment. I must tell you my foundation and what has led me to this point so that I can connect with you exactly where you have been, where you are, or where life leads you next. To go through everything that I had been through, to get to this point, and still find peace, strength, love, and happiness in my process was not easy. It was my anchor that kept me grounded.

If you want to build something impactful, you need a solid foundation. I cannot tell you where your foundation should begin. I was raised on faith in God and resting in believing that he has a plan for all of us. The anchor that I wear today is in the form of a handmade necklace. My anchor reminds me that everything I have lived and the strength that I have endured will continue to carry me, no matter how massive the tides of water are. Life is a never-ending journey with many ups and downs. The place our faith lives will be where we will gain strength in each chapter along the way.

Before you understood your sport, you had to build on your foundation: the fundamentals. I don't know about you, but when I was younger, I felt like the fundamentals began to get repetitive. It wasn't until I started noticing my progress that I realized the fundamentals are required to build on your game and advance to another level. Your confidence is in your fundamentals. It has shown you ultimate faith and trust in yourself and your abilities. Over time, you begin to see that your foundation has become a part of your habits in progress.

I was fortunate to play basketball at every level. I tell people all of the time that I have been playing since my mother's womb. My mother was still playing basketball while five months pregnant with me.

She did not have an opportunity of being a college athlete and a young single mother. Knowing that we both played for the same high school still amazes me.

High School Opened My Eyes

You might ask, well, who is PATRINA GOREE? TRINA GOREE? Where did she play? My journey was quite an adventure and still is today. I will begin in high school. Believe it or not, I did not start playing organized basketball until I was a freshman in high school. I found out the definition of what JV and Varsity meant when I arrived on campus. I had never played AAU summer basketball until my sophomore year. All of this was foreign to me because I was only used to playing in the neighborhood parks and imitating what I saw from watching college, WNBA, and NBA basketball. I was a true fan and student of the game. I would watch the television for hours to learn who the players, coaches, and commentators were on each level. The game came naturally to me, but I was so passive when I started with a team. I focused more on learning how to play the game because there is a big difference between recreation and organized sports.

I was a varsity player at Jack Yates High School in Houston. My high school career-high, in points, may have been anywhere between 12-15 points. I earned 2nd team all-conference my junior year and 1st team all-conference my senior year. I was not a star player. I was cool with playing my role. At my high school, being able to represent and play at the varsity level was almost every 3rd ward (neighborhood in Houston) kids dream. My school motto is pride, excellence, and tradition.

I want to briefly honor our 2008-2009 and 2009-2010 boys' basketball team as they were ranked number 1 in the nation and back to back state champions. Those guys do not get enough recognition as they set a standard of excellence in athletics. That was an exciting time to be in high school as our girls' team were also in pursuit.

Being on the girls' basketball team, we were undefeated my senior year but came up short by losing a game that would get us to the state tournament. Once again, I was not a star player, but I was a starter and one of the best defenders on our team. I lacked confidence and would overthink instead of relying on my instincts. A lot of that had to do with me inserting myself in the system, being undersized in position, and still learning how to play with a team. It was not hard. We played an up-tempo game, so my job would be to defend and run the floor to make layups. It's when the playoffs would come around that I realized that I was smaller in matchups, but I always played like I was big. Overthinking would not allow me to play free. I wanted to be my best so bad that I kept thinking that I would eventually rise to that greatness, instead of making that moment in time my best day.

All I knew was that I wanted to play college basketball but did not have a clue about the recruiting process and how everything worked. I thought that going to college would be like high school: Apply for the school and try out for the basketball team. I was wrong. I was on my way to becoming a first-generation college student with minimal guidance. I never fully expressed my desire to play at the next level with my high school coach, so I don't think he knew how serious I was. No one around me could help because they were focused on trying to make a living and had never been in my situation.

Toward the end of my senior year, athletes were beginning to sign letters of intent to colleges to continue football, basketball, and track. I was still in the process of figuring out how to get an opportunity at college. At the time, all I did was apply to schools. Again, I thought that was all I had to do.

Welcome to College

Entering college, I did not have a clue about how college athletics worked. I did not have help in making a sound decision on where I should spend the next four years of my life (or 1st year of college in my case). Looking back, all I had to do was ask a few people who possibly knew about the college process to see how it worked. All I knew was that I wanted to get far away from home and what I was used to seeing. I also thought that it would be super cool for my family and friends to talk about how far away I was. Being a first-generation college student, I wanted to be an example for my family and friends, so there was no pressure.

I decided to attend was a 4-year private school in New Mexico. I did minimal research and saw that we would, at least, play some schools in Texas, so I could have a few people to support me. I remember filling out the women's basketball questionnaire that would go directly to the head coach. He called me late in the summer and offered me a $1,500 scholarship for the year. Now keep in mind, I'm a first-generation college student-athlete, all I wanted to do was play basketball. What did I do? I accepted the offer, verbally. Yes, only $1,500.

By August, I arrived on campus one week early. My early arrival allowed me to get situated, meet teammates, my coach, the place I would spend the next year of my life, and register for classes. At registration, that's when things got real for me. I learned that to be a collegiate athlete, you must be a full-time student.

Full time was about five classes per week that were 3 hours each. That means that one course would be on Monday, Wednesday, and Friday for 1 hour per day. That was not an issue with me. The problem was that for that semester alone, I had a balance of $10,000: $20,000 for the year. I was distraught. The coach told me that I would have a $1,500 scholarship. That was only $750 per semester. I did not know anything about college and the financial business of things. I assume that most people don't. What I learned in this process is that there are also levels in scholarships. Some people get full, partial, athletic, and academic scholarship awards. Being out of state did not help with out-of-state fees.

Hearing $20,000 made me panic! The $1,500 scholarship was not enough, but I was grateful for the opportunity and the award. As for the remainder of the balance, who was going to cover this? How would this fee be paid? I arrived from 3rd ward on a hope and a dream. $10,000 was just not feasible. I knew I could not go back home and feel disappointed and have to explain this situation. I had approximately $100 in my pocket. That was not going to cut the cost by a long shot!

The academic advisor talked to me about loan options. I had always heard people warn students to stay away from loans if possible. It was like cynicism, in a sense. Loans were like sins the way people talked about it. Being in New Mexico, I could not just go back home. I was making my first adult decision that was far away from home, without any trusted help. I wanted to embrace being a college athlete.

I remember witnessing my new teammates and other students with their parents, helping them make all of the decisions in which I had many questions to ask. I was embarrassed. I felt alone but kept a calm demeanor. I began to think to try to make something happen. My hustler's instinct kicked in. I had a few resources to make some decisions.

A program that I was a part of in high school awarded me a $4,000 scholarship. As long as I attended four years of college, I was guaranteed $500 per semester as a full-time student. Being a low-income household student and independent granted me the $5,000 federal grant: $2,500 per semester. With the deductions, I still owed $10,000 per semester. The college was a private institution, so the fees were through the roof!

	Fall 2010	Spring 2011
Tuition / Housing / Other	13,750	13,750
Federal Grants	- 2,500	- 2,500
Basketball Scholarship	- 750	- 750
High School Program	- 500	- 500
Remaining Balance	10,000	10,000

I remember taking out a $20,000 loan that year alone: unsubsidized and subsidized. I'm not advising anyone to do this. I did not know anything about the financial or student-athlete process in college. Still, I do not regret my journey one bit. I would recommend you look into every option and avenue before making a decision and investment in yourself and your goals. You should never be afraid to take a step back and evaluate your process and where you are.
In this case, I bet on my anchor.

You may think that you do not have time or feel delayed but always be patient on your journey. Little did I know, colleges were cheaper back home and would always be there. If someone would have told me that you do not have to attend college immediately after high school as an athlete, I don't know what decision I would have made. I took the best route in the position that I stood. I knew one thing for sure after signing up for that loan, I could not and would not be attending that school the following year. Once I made my decision, I looked forward and felt a release of pressure. It was time to focus on what I went there to do, which was play basketball.

Being a freshman in college was mentally tough. There are things that people can talk to you about, but you can only prepare for those experiences when you're in the situation. My freshman year coach decided to make a JV team. I had never heard of colleges branching into JV teams. I thought that was only in high school. Initially, I was upset, angry, and felt disrespected. I felt played like a video game. I felt like I was starting from the bottom again. I was embarrassed to tell people this, in fear that they would consider this a downgrade. This situation gave me more of an edge and chip on my shoulder. I wanted to prove that I was better than what I projected as disrespect from the coach and team.

The JV squad turned out to be my blessing in disguise and made me aware that everything does happen for a reason. I had the opportunity to compete against some of the top junior college teams in the region. Some of those teams were nationally ranked. These girls I competed against were better than the girls I had to battle at the school. I could have given up, but it was my anchor that kept me grounded. Besides, I had just committed to a $20,000 student loan.

After my first game, I noticed different recruiters and college coaches from division 1 programs in attendance. I was glad to have been on JV. I was the leader in points, steals, and assists per game. No hype: I probably averaged over 20 points per game. Those statistics are not online. I began to understand that college athletics had different levels and classifications.

By the end of my freshman year, I saw that some of my high school classmates were beginning to transfer schools as well or ended up back home for their reasons. I began to put myself out there. I knew that if I wanted to continue playing basketball and at a higher level, I would need to transfer. I reached out to every junior college coach in the state of Texas. I knew that I could play because I was playing at a high level whenever I faced those junior college teams. All of the schools that I knew I played well against, I reached out to their coaches first. My logic in this process was that these coaches had witnessed me playing at a high level and saw my character firsthand.

All but one college turned down my request for a tryout because they had their rosters filled or did not have any scholarships available. I was not settling for anything less in my sophomore year after pulling out a $20,000 loan. My goal was free education and doing what I love. I knew that I was going to secure this opportunity because my mindset shifted, and I rested in my anchor.

Going home in the summer gave me more time to evaluate and conclude that I would be going to a different school. Every day, I trained and worked on my game. I knew I had gotten better because every time I went to an open gym, the game started to make more sense. I was still figuring things out, but I had my first year under my belt in playing the point guard position primarily. I had a different motor about myself.

Junior College

Coach N. from a junior college, in Texas, granted me a private workout. This tryout was destiny meeting me again but leading me into another direction. Not only was I requesting a private workout but negotiating a full scholarship. I understood my worth and who I was, in the most respectful way. I think God was testing my anchor and wanted to see if I would take the necessary steps in going after what I wanted.

I asked one of my good friends, Toad, to travel to the school with me. At the end of the tryout, Coach N. explained that he was looking for a post player. I'm a guard. I immediately thought, to myself, that I wasted my time after he assisted me through several drills and took my friend and me to lunch. While we were at lunch and reflecting on the workout, the coach started telling me about his assistant coach from the previous season. She had accepted a position as the head coach at a junior college in Oklahoma. He said that she needed one more guard to complete her team. He told me that he signed a good group of guards but thanked me for coming to his tryout and that he appreciated my hard work.

After eating, Coach N. wished us a safe trip back to Houston and told me that he would be in contact with me. On the way back to Houston, Toad and I discussed having a gut feeling of Coach N. bringing me in to evaluate my workout for his former assistant coach. I learned that your energy introduces you and speak for you when things are good and when things look uncertain. It is so important to be the very best version of yourself, even when things are blurry.

I followed up with Coach N. about one week later. He told me, once again, that he did not have a position available for me on his team, but he will forward me his former assistants' phone number. He said that she would be expecting my phone call. I called his former assistant, Coach T. She told me that a girl she was recruiting decided not to sign and that she had one full scholarship available for that year. In brief, she said that the award was mine if I wanted to go to be a student-athlete at Eastern Oklahoma State College.

Full scholarship? That was my language and the goal I had set for myself. She asked for my email address. After signing, I would need to fax it immediately. I took care of business and felt overwhelmed with joy. Right after talking to Coach T., I called Coach N. and thanked him for allowing me to try out for him. He wished me luck. Fate and destiny were evident. It's crazy because I didn't think I would be going back out of state, after trying to land a spot on a junior college team in Texas.

I had gone from needing a $20,000 loan, precisely one year prior, to a full scholarship. Not only did I get the scholarship award for the year, but I conducted my first business deal, in hindsight. I was building the relationship, networking, and created a business deal that could become a lifelong partnership. That partnership is that Coach T. is a family member, to me, for life. Still, in this present day, we are in touch. She knows how much I appreciate her. She was more than a basketball coach.

The love that Coach T. spreads is real. Usually, players would go on visits to check out the school, organization, and get a vibe for the coaches and team with their parents. Those options are what I like to call luxuries. I didn't have that kind of luxury. I signed from home, no visit, didn't know what the team looked like, and didn't know Coach T. beyond that one conversation.

All in all, I was in the right position because I stood firm on my anchor. Sometimes the situation is not what it looks like initially for many players. My case was trustworthy and thorough with her. She did not sugar coat anything; she always kept it real, and never sold a false reality within her program.

Having a coach that genuinely does care for their players off of the court is so refreshing. The presence of this coach taught me so much. Not every coach can connect with you and understand you on a level more profound than the game. They can say they do, but you can tell, depending on the circumstances. Building relationships are so meaningful in life. Never choose an opportunity because it looks golden. Most times, you have to place yourself in the position of where you want to be. Wherever you are led from your anchor, just sure you make your mark and leave your legacy.

You would think that it was smooth sailing with my transition to my new school. After the first pre-season tournament, I was ready to throw in the towel. Never in my life had I felt like this. I performed terrible, trying to find my identity within the team. I went back to practice, refocused and turned up. I had to accept that I was becoming the go-to player of a team for the first time in my life. I wasn't the best player, but I outworked everybody. Coach T. will tell you that herself. By the best, I mean, I didn't have the best all-around game, but I was the best and go-to player. The team relied on me in a significant way, as I had a different responsibility, a different role. I was a scorer. If a bucket was needed, there was no distrust in my mind that I would make something happen.

At mid-season, I was on the ranks in our region. I averaged 14 points per game, three rebounds and steals per game, and four assists per game. I was having the time of my life and the confidence to go to another level. I had a division 2 school in Georgia show their interest. I found my way at junior college. I embraced what it was like being one of the top players.

The love was different on campus and in the community. It just showed me that this game would give you what you give to it, especially if you are in the best situation for you. I gave the game all of my love and passion. I received it back. By no means did I ever feel entitled. I knew that my hard work was paying off. My confidence was going to another level, and I remained humble because I never forgot my roots.

Division 1 Basketball

Going into the summer before my junior year, I was back at square one, even after what I believed to be a successful season in college. I remember going back home. I risked it all that summer. I stayed focus on improving my game and being ready for an opportunity. I turned the volume up on my workouts by doing 2-mile morning runs, lifting light weights, and even shooting 500 jump shots per day. In the mornings, before the basketball courts would fill up, I also ran fast-break full-court drills. I did personal 2-a-days for training.

I could not believe where I was. At this point, the schools that were interested in me, either the coaches resigned or did not give me an offer. No one tells you or warn you about these things. It's not something you think about while playing. That summer, I was invited for a workout at a division 2 school in New Mexico. I went out there and killed the workout. I was already putting in the work, and my confidence was on another level.

No disrespect, but by the end of the workout, the coach knew that I was a good basketball player. She offered me a walk-on position. I felt disrespected after I pulled my resources together to be able to travel there and was at the top of my game. With my previous season, knowing the value that I displayed, I knew that I wasn't settling to walk-on. During that workout and basketball hoop session, I killed everybody and showed my skills at a high level. I absolutely would not be content for a walk-on position, especially at a division 2 school, when my goal was the higher level. I thanked the coach for the opportunity but respectfully declined that offer.

It was three weeks before a new school year was to begin. I still had no interest letters, no scholarship offers, and no solid plan on where I was going. One day, I woke up with so much confidence. I was bold. I decided to do something completely crazy! I emailed the coach at Texas Southern University, division 1, in my neighborhood. Their coach at the time is a WNBA Hall of Famer.

My email was requesting a meeting to get a few minutes of her time. My goal was to get on the team no matter what the obstacles were.

Initially, I emailed her about ten times before she finally responded to me. I was very determined, and this was kind of far-fetched, although the school was right in my neighborhood. In one of her responses, she said that she already had several point guards and was not looking for another. She followed up that she would be in her office the following week.

I thought to myself, "This coach would not be replying to me if there were no window of opportunity when stating she would be in her office. She is not looking for another point guard, but she also had not seen me or what I could bring to her team."

I replied and told her that I understood that she was at point guard capacity and gave her a day and time frame that I could meet at her office. Could you imagine the nerves I had the day it was time to have my meeting and speak for myself? I prepared to showcase my skills and why I knew I could be an asset to play on this level and with her team. My mentality was not personal to anybody but myself! I knew where I came from and where I wanted to go. I had to be bold in my approach. Boldness would determine the difference between how I started in high school to where I am now. Every level requires another level of confidence in yourself.

After the meeting, she offered me an opportunity to walk-on. Of course, I accepted this. She said that it was a 2-week trial before finalizing the roster spot. Then she linked me with one of the assistant coaches who would help me complete my class schedule to fit with practice times. I had to go through the NCAA compliance guidelines and steps. I had not made it on the team just yet, but I was ready to begin pre-season workouts the following week.

Every practice, every workout, every opportunity, I displayed my best. If point guards had to run the full length of the court in 12 seconds, I pushed to shave my time by 2 seconds. I was wide awake at 4:45 am practices while others were still trying to wake up. My mentality was to outwork everybody, every single day, and every single second. I'm not blowing any smoke. Again, my grind was not personal to anybody but myself.

You would be surprised at the people who said I was not good enough to play on the division 1 level. If I could pull out a $20,000 loan to play my freshman year, I could sacrifice a smaller loan to play on a higher level. The student loan may have only been $5,000, for the year, to cover other expenses. I knew what my dreams and goals were. I knew my anchor. I did not focus on what could go wrong when everything in my control (working out, getting better, networking) was working for me.

The 2-week trial came and left. The coach never announced that I made it, I just continued to practice and stayed committed. This season was short-lived for me. Nonetheless, this coach taught me a lot on the court and off of the court. Every day I got better. She knew the game. She understood how to bring out the best in her players. I learned how to understand coaches and their philosophies. A coach can only teach you what they know. This woman knew the game inside out. In the time I spent on this team, I continued to get better.

Senior Year

Going into my senior year of college, I transferred schools. The same school that I went to the prior summer, for a workout, in New Mexico, decided to offer me their full scholarship. The coaches found out that I was playing at a high level the previous season, knew about the situation of my removal from the team, and didn't hesitate to send me the offer. That's when I learned never to place too much value in other people's opinions because, a year before, I was offered a "walk-on" role, at best, from the same coaches, from this same school. No disrespect, but I knew my value. I was grateful but felt downgraded and did not put as much emphasis on the grind after being months removed from the game. The season started very rough for me before it got better. This year, in general, was just a whole life learning experience.

No one told me that if I transferred to another division 1, I could have a redshirt year and still have two more years of eligibility. That move would have probably given me a mental break to get my confidence back to where it was after I left Texas Southern University. By moving to a division 2 school, I had access to play right away. The downfall is that I would be considered a senior despite only playing in one game the prior season. I was upset because I was already in this new situation. I'm not blaming the coaches or anybody for this situation. I was more upset because I just did not know about all of these rules before signing the dotted lines.

Days before the season opener, I was performing well in practices but fell to an injury. I found myself with a bruised knee. I had to sit out for one month. At that time, I was distracted. Basketball was the last thing that my mind was on. This season killed the passion that once existed. I went through a lot, on and off of the court.

By transferring to so many schools, for basketball, I did not graduate at the end of my senior year. With different schools offering different degree plans, the credits didn't align. I was not on track to receive a bachelor's degree at the end of my senior year. I had no goal and became lost. I did not know what was next for me. It seemed like basketball was beginning to take off when I was on my journey with junior college and then became a blur immediately after.

My college basketball career did not end how I expected it to, so I decided to go back home to complete my bachelor's degree. I had earned my associate degree from junior college, but I knew that wasn't going to be enough. I made up in my mind that I wanted to finish what I started since I only attended college to play basketball. I felt that I had to complete my education to have something to show for my college experience.

Professional Basketball

Although I focused on school, I never stopped working on my basketball game. One day, the scout for the Harlem Globetrotters reached out to my mentor. The next thing I know, she asked if I wanted to try out for them. It wasn't my dream to play for them, but I knew this opportunity would allow me to continue playing.

"Foreal? The Globetrotters? Okay, yeah, that would be cool."

I wasn't nonchalant. I just didn't think too far into it. I knew that this was a legendary organization. Opportunities like this are rare and hard to come by, so why not? It wouldn't hurt me to try out. Besides, I had been working on my game every day to be ready for an opportunity.

I was in my head for a moment like "I don't know any of those tricks, what if they ask me to do tricks? Can I at least spin the ball? I could dribble the basketball. I know how to shoot. Tricks? We will see." I remember that night before the tryout. I was trying to spin the ball in my apartment and trying not to look goofy if they were to ask if I could spin the ball with my finger.

During the tryout, I don't think it registered to me that I was trying out for the Harlem Globetrotters. The coaches put me and some guys through ball-handling drills (that didn't include tricks yet) and brought in one of the women who were already on the team. I got a chance to talk with her and watch how she worked. I paid close attention to what she was doing and thought, "Wow, she's awesome."

Then one of the coaches asked me, "Do you think you can do that?" That's the moment I realized that I was trying out for the Globetrotters. I said, "Yeah, I think I can do that, coach."

Ready.

Set.

Go.

I began to do what I saw. The coach was impressed and saw something in me. He asked me to do different things about 30 or 40 times. The more I kept doing it, the more I started having fun. I was feeling like a Globetrotter at that moment. All of what I panicked about the night before takes respect, repetition, and attention to detail. He started showing me film of current and former players and I began to fall in love with this possibility.

After the tryout, I felt a shift in my mood. I was excited again. I thought I made it when the coaches told me that they would be in contact with me. I thought I was just waiting on the call to leave the next day. At the time, I was working a day job. I was so exhausted, my body was sore, and all I could think was that I couldn't wait to play for them. I could see myself doing what I love full time. God has a funny way of distributing patience, though.

One of the coaches would check in with me from time to time and ask if I had been working on those things. I was. I didn't go anywhere without my basketball at that time. After three months, I finally learned how to spin the ball with confidence and without feeling goofy. Everything I worked on took a lot of faith, patience, time, blood, sweat, more patience, uncertainty, just everything. Although this was an exciting time, I will never discredit the hard work it takes to do these things. I will always respect everything and everyone before me and currently.

After eight months of my initial try out, I received my invitation to mini-camp in Philadelphia. During the camp, we played some games and practiced their skills and drills. It was three other women and me along with a lot of the guys. Everything happened so fast. It was so much to soak in. I just could not believe it. I had a lot of emotions going on. I was excited, nervous, happy, and clueless, but I put my best foot forward and continued to trust this new process.

After the mini-camp, I flew back to my home base in Houston. I left Philly with uncertainty but hope. As requested, "Keep working on your game. We will be in touch." It was still a waiting game. Time continued to pass, and although I kept working on my game, I began to get discouraged. Official training camp had started, and I did not receive this invitation. At that point, I felt that the journey was over. There was something in me that I did not understand.

All this time, I did not understand why, but I kept working on everything I learned and my game. Even while discouraged, I kept pressing forward and kept praying about it because it did not make any sense to me that I kept working. I downloaded Sweet Georgia Brown and placed myself in position as a Globetrotter. I had some support, but some family members did not believe me and started to think I was crazy.

One day, I was talking to my cousin, Jazzy, about this whole process. We were headed to the park to run the trail. After I reached my mile run, I still had my basketball with me. As I came to a stop, my cousin and I were talking, and I was spinning my basketball. Suddenly, a guy was running in the opposite direction, with BIG headphones on, and he began to whistle Sweet Georgia Brown. That's the Globetrotter song. How crazy was that? He did not stop to talk or anything. I kid you not.

Me: Jazz, you heard that?

Jazz: Girl, what?

Me: Yo, did you hear him whistling the Globetrotter song?

Jazz: Oh, Foreal?

She had no clue where my mind was. She didn't even know the song. I was in my world, simply trying to figure out what that meant. Was it a sign? A week later, I had a dream that I was in a Harlem Globetrotter uniform. I was getting ready for a game, and my teammates (who didn't have a face in my dream) were like, "Yo, you're ready, relax!"

Maybe two weeks later, which was about a year after my initial tryout, I got a phone call presented with an opportunity to leave within a couple of days. I departed a week later. I felt like I began to work on everything as if I were in overtime in a game. I celebrated, I cried tears of joy, and this moment started to make sense. I arrived expecting to practice, and in two days, I was already on the floor playing. I had been to a different city every night and had played in various colleges and NBA arenas.

The opportunity that I was fortunate to have with the Harlem Globetrotters was once in a lifetime. At the time, there had only been 13 women who were a part of the organization. I was considered a taxi player, meaning that I was not under a contract. During my time with them, the organization was in its' 90th year. It's amazing how I met the first woman who played for the Harlem Globetrotters when I played AAU basketball in my sophomore year of high school.

I never saw myself as a Globetrotter before getting an opportunity to try out. Being a part of history is a beautiful feeling. Not many people, in fact, women, can gain experience in that uniform. I say with pride that I am thankful, and my experience was terrific. You have to trust your process because no matter how long it lasts, the journey is beautiful.

I wanted that experience to last forever, but it did not. I was so determined to continue playing basketball and decided not to wait on an agent. I knew that I was not going to get anywhere by waiting on someone to speak on my behalf, who had no clue who I was. I started to take matters into my own hands and rely on my anchor.

I saw that every resource was accessible online with social media and the internet. I researched teams, coaches, and players of organizations to find in different countries. I would type my pitch in a language translator and send the email or direct messages to them. After numerous rejections or lack of responses from other countries, I zoned in on Mexico and the LMBPF League.

Having a Mexican friend from the gym where I worked, changed the game for me. Sending messages and emails to the coaches, team pages, and players was working. One of the coaches in Mexico contacted me back via direct messages and sent me his phone number. I let my friend talk on my behalf, like an agent, and was on my way to Mexico City within one week.

I lived there for about three months with a room, daily meals, and no pay. My objective was to build my professional resume, even if that meant starting over and from zero. It didn't take more than $10-$15 U.S. Dollars per week to live in Mexico with a free room and food. The world was different there and a total cultural shock.

Most people had their businesses on the first floor of their homes. There was food on every block, at all times of the day and night. Families still hand washed and dried their clothing with Hayneedle outdoors. There are no lines for the lanes in the streets.

After Mexico, I reevaluated my process and where I was. I realized that I was still chasing the high of the feeling I had when I played for the Harlem Globetrotters. I experienced what I would call PTSD and trying to find my identity and who I was without the game of basketball. The game was why I lived. I could not see myself doing anything but playing basketball, and I was not ready to leave the game. I could not picture my life being different than it was a year prior. I had gone from getting paid to play this game to being desperate and playing for free, accepting free housing and meals. I went from playing in front of thousands of fans, making people smile, and feeling valued to making $10/hour at a gym and then playing for free in a foreign country.

When I went back home, I was embarrassed for people to see me making a living, working in a gym. Sadly, it never mattered. I decided to spend time with my cousin in San Diego and used this time and space to search through my soul. I wanted to discover who I was without the game of basketball. I practiced Tai Chi and Yoga. Both practices brought me to a state of being present. It gave me present peace and made me zone in on my present moment. It taught me gratitude for life in my past, present, and future.

Nothing around me mattered. The only thing that existed was being present. My thoughts went out of the window, my mind state shifted, and there was peace. Having the courage to practice self-care and patience played a significant role in my being.

By the end of that year, 2017, I decided that it was time to do something different if I wanted to play professional basketball. I was down to no other option, still working at a gym, so I decided to return to school to earn my master's degree. Here we go again: It was basketball that sent me back to school. I decided to go to graduate school because if I could use a loan to play in college, I could use a loan to invest in my dream. I did the master's program online and had to become a full-time student for that benefit of requesting a loan.

I planned to find a team that I could play for in a country that spoke some English to make things easier for me. Nothing was easy about my plan. I contacted teams and coaches in Australia and told them that I would be there in February of 2018. During my time there, my goal would be to try out for all of the organizations that were willing to let me showcase my skills. Some of the coaches replied and told me that they looked forward to me arriving in Australia. Others did not respond. I knew that they would be easier to contact when I visited.

The day came when it was time for me to go to the country down under. Everything you could think of went wrong. I arrived at the airport with my passport and was ready to go. At check-in, the ticket agent told me that I needed a visa permit to get to Australia at bag check-in. He told me it would take approximately 20 minutes to process. By the time I purchased the visa online and waited on the process to be approved, and showed the ticket agent, he told me that I could not check-in due to the gate closing. I was late according to international baggage check-in within those 20 minutes. My thoughts were all over the place. I was upset that he didn't tell me this before processing my visa. I felt defeated. I kept begging and pleading him to let me into the security check-in. Still, he was persistent in not following my command.

I refused to leave the airport. I felt like there was no way that I went through all of the trouble. To enroll in school, attend full-time online, and not continue professional basketball was not going to be a waste. I felt low.

I called two people on my phone to help me find solutions to the madness. My sister put her foot down and called my bank to dispute the plane ticket I paid for since I could not get on my flight. One of my best friends gave me her credit card information and told me to purchase a one-way ticket. I gave her one-third of the money right away with a digital transaction. I promised to have the remainder as soon as I arrived home. I kept my promise and was on my way to Australia.

Having real friends who believe in you and your goals is hard to find. She showed me that she knew what I was working on and saw my vision beyond the surface of just wanting to go to Australia to play basketball. She labeled this move, ICONIC. That made me feel like there was no way that I could let this opportunity pass. I got tired of waiting for agents, coaches, and teams. I trusted in God, who was my anchor. I had crazy faith. I reversed the script and leaped in the hope of having the first line of connection.

It's different when you represent yourself. You have to make sure you know who you are, your anchor, and why you are doing what you are doing. You have to sell yourself. I figured that I could speak on my behalf, market myself, and build those relationships myself. Waiting on a middleman, who did not know anything about me, was not enough in my situation.

My resume spoke volumes, but I did not have the statistics to back me up. I'm not recommending my story; I'm only sharing the experience of how my journey unfolded. Being in and out of the game, physically, has always put me last. I was never looking for worldly recognition and profile. Having my anchor and having a "go" always kept me ahead of the business game.

My travel time was 42 hours. Houston to Taipei was a 16-hour flight. I had a 17-hour layover in Taipei. Taipei to Brisbane, Australia, was another 9 hours. When I made it to Australia, once again, another problem had occurred. My transportation app did not work. I had to catch a cab to the gym. I told one of the coaches that I would report directly to the gym when I arrived. When I arrived, it was time to pay, and my debit card would not go through. I had the funds on my debit card, but the card did not work. I had to call home and ask my mother if she could send me her card info so that I could make the payment. I would send her the money back as soon as I got the situation handled. I did not think to inform my bank that I would be out of the country. Small things make a huge difference.

The first coach I did a tryout for, put me in business mode. Not only was I a player that was looking for an opportunity, but I was representing myself. I was my agent. The coach wanted to get to know me. He asked me who I was and what goal was I looking to accomplish while in Australia. He introduced me to his staff and told me that I could get some days of individual training with some of the men and women players. Before this tryout, the only sleep I had was on the plane. The coach noticed that the lack of rest did not stop my pursuit.

After the tryout, I arrived at my room. There was a restaurant connected to the apartments. I stepped in to order a croissant sandwich (knowing that my card was temporarily not working). Before the owner told me my total, we were having a conversation. I was telling her what brought me to Australia and my journey with basketball. She noticed my accent and knew that I was foreign. The sandwich had finished, and it was time to slide my card. I played it off by looking confused, but she kept attempting to charge my card for the purchase. Finally, she gave up and told me that the croissant would be my welcome to Australia. It was then that my journey to Australia became an enormous investment that I made for my career.

During my first week in Brisbane, I found myself on a date with a guy who played basketball as well. He showed me the town, took me to his church, and welcomed me with fun times and frozen yogurt. Of everything that I planned, it was honestly refreshing to have this spontaneity to enjoy the country without being overwhelmed in business. There are some things that you cannot make a plan for in life.

I knew that being in Australia was an excellent move for where I was in my career.

Every day that I was there, I got acclimated to the Australian dialect and culture. The people that I came into contact with were accommodating and friendly. I pictured myself there, living my best life. After several workouts for different teams, there were some factors beyond my control that would not permit me to receive a contract and continue my career in Australia.

I suddenly felt an overwhelming peace after knowing that I put my best foot forward in everything that I could control. I played at the top of my game. I set up a personal tour to showcase my talent and market myself. After receiving emails from coaches, I knew that I had given the game everything that I had. I was declined contracts from factors that were not in my control. There was peace in my heart, knowing that I didn't have any more to give to the game. It was time for me to pay it forward.

A few months after retiring my basketball shoes, I received a job opportunity that would lead me into a world I could not imagine for years to come. I was fortunate for this job because it confirmed that my time to transition was happening. My heart was in the right place. I was ready to experience a new journey and receive all that God had in store for me.

I have practiced every tool in this book, from playing sports to working in the sports industry. Life is short. I hope that you give your game everything you have so that when you transition, you will find the peace in your heart in knowing that you are going to be okay because you have everything that you need. If you are no longer active in your sport, I hope you can find peace, if you have not. Use the tools you have gained through your game to unlock your purpose into your present.

Remember that you are only competing against yourself and that you never have to prove anything to anyone. Live your best life. However, you define it. Be kind to yourself as well as others. Always be fearless in any opportunity. Never work for money but work for experience and happiness, and you will never lack. The money will come, just like it goes. Be patient and present in your journey. Believe in YOU!

Time Out

We cannot control the future, but we can take ownership of our journey and create our narrative. We can't control the past because it's far behind. Everything that you have been through will prepare you if you just believe it. Take a deep breath.

Take Action

- Reflect on your journey.
- What is your anchor?
- What is your story?
- Do you let others write your narrative, or do you take ownership of your why?

IDENTITY HUNT

"Who Am I?"

2

"The act of discovering who we are will force us to accept that we can go further than we think."

-PAULO COELHO

(Coelho, 1993).

You may have been participating in your sport all of your life, or you may just be getting started. Either way, it's easy to get caught up in your athletic identity, with it being the majority of your lifestyle representation. You enjoy the feeling of people on the outside of your everyday life, recognizing that you are an athlete. You don't think about this, but you do. It almost feels like the jackpot when someone guesses the exact sport that you play. On the flip side, it can get offensive when people place stereotypes on athletes. You know that you are more than an athlete, but do others truly view you for being more? They probably don't and likely will. That is okay.

While in school, no one realizes how hard you have to study and focus on academics to excel. There are requirements on all levels, in grade school and college, that all athletes must meet to participate in their sports. Many people think that it's easy because they believe that professors automatically pass athletes. I have never been in that situation. I always thought that my professors were harder on us, and I would hear this coming from my teammates as well. We thought professors would give us a break with trying to balance academics and athletics, but that was never the case. No sympathy because there are students with full-time jobs. The only difference is the job of a student-athlete requires frequent travel.

Not all student-athletes have other people do their homework for them. People assume that study hall and having a tutor is because student-athletes cannot keep up with the curriculum in their classes. Study hall is where coaches carve out time for the athlete to stay on track within their courses and remain eligible. They can have tutors to ensure that student-athletes are not missing assignments. As an athlete, you lose a lot of time in the classroom with being on the road and playing multiple games. There are no excuses at all. One of the first life lessons thrown upon an athlete is time management.

Not all student-athletes will major in a sports-related degree plan. Everyone does not want to work in sports after playing. Not all athletes want to become coaches because "it seems fitting." We know what we put our coaches through and the challenges they go through daily, beyond sports. Not all female athletes are lesbians (no offense). Women just love what we do, and if we're good at sports, it doesn't make us masculine. Not all male athletes are ladies' men. Not all athletes have poor money management. These are things I've heard people talk about and read that are biased. I just don't think people can label you without truly understanding who you are. And even so, they should be more focused on your characteristics and who you are.

Self-Awareness

Blocking out the noise that surrounds you is critical in your development. Take constructive criticism and apply it where there's truth. You cannot rely on others to search for your meaning and discover who you are because only you can answer the deep questions about yourself. You must be completely honest with yourself when building your identity. Assessing where you are, your strengths, and where you want to be, has to come from within yourself. You are on a scavenger hunt once you go to the other side of sports. In my opinion, the scavenger hunt is less about what you want to do next in life but more about discovering who you are so that you'll know what you need. There is no one-size-fits-all, step-by-step process in building your identity.

For instance, a sports facility and a restaurant are both built from a foundation. The common factor is that both establishments serve a purpose. The difference is that although the foundations are similar in construction from ground level, the sports facility is to meet the needs of athletics and wellness. There may be equipment on the floor, a basketball court, and rubber tiles to protect the members' bone joints. The restaurant may not need much thought into the flooring. They just need to accommodate guests to be seated and the workspace of the employees who are cooking and serving.

The sports facility does not function the same way that a restaurant would. On the surface, they are both only buildings that serve a purpose. No one, except the owner, cares what it took to gain establishment and present a well-operated facility. The owners are on the front line of care when it comes to the maintenance and upkeep of their establishments. They know that no matter how great the building looks on the outside, the loyal consumers only care about what's inside. To compete in their markets, the owners must know that their business model should start with their purpose of why their establishments exist.

Given this, other doors open for the owners with expansion, partnerships, sponsorships, and other business ventures.

As athletes, our projection of expression, through our sports, is a part of our brand. You are the owner of your brand establishment, and you exist for a purpose. No one will truly understand the DNA of being an athlete unless they come through that journey. Your advantage, in life after sports, is that all of the foundational work that happens in your athletic development will transfer in every aspect. The maintenance of the principles (hustle, heart, discipline, resilience, etc.) that you gained along the way will carry you into the person you want to become. The inside work must be handled with self-love and self-care while on your identity hunt and maintaining your brand.

No one knows or cares about what it takes to rebuild your identity because others are busy focusing on their self-discoveries. All people see is what they assume is a finished product of your current situation. Don't judge yourself. Doors will open for you if you always tap into yourself. If you stay patient and know that you are not alone, your patience and purpose will bring you balance.

Learn Something New

When I transitioned into the corporate world, I had to prove my worth beyond what I had identified as my whole life: an athlete. Granted, I wouldn't have gotten this far without my athletic background. Knowing who I am today holds more weight than talking about what I did. During my first interview, the person who became my manager asked, "I understand that you know the game of basketball, but do you know the business?" It was like she asked a question that turned into a wakeup call.

That moment gave me something to ponder. I was 26 years old and thought I had a general idea about the business of sports. Considering my sports journey and everything I went through as a player, I felt that I knew what was going on in the sports industry. I did not. I was not clueless, but I was just like the rest of the world. I could only see it for as far as I was physically involved. It's a different microscope when you study the game as a player and then wear a business hat and look at it from that perspective. The business is the total operation of an organization, not just the actual game. The game is a significant factor but only one element of the organization.

One of the first things I learned was that I needed to separate myself from being just an athlete and turn into a businesswoman, quick. When I say businesswoman, I'm talking about beyond sports in this example as well. So, what did I do?

- Instead of dressing casually in the office, I continued to wear business attire or business casual clothes. You never know who you will run into, so you always want to present your best self. You are your first impression of your brand.

- I was assertive and spoke to every person I saw and introduced myself as "Trina Goree." I was genuine and did this with a smile. It was that simple.

Learning and knowing who we are is in alliance with what we do. What we do is not precisely who we are. If titles, accolades, and worldly status did not exist, would you know who you are? If the very thing or sport that you identify yourself with was to leave you tomorrow, how would you define or introduce yourself?

I wanted people to know more about what kind of person I was instead of solely relying on my active status to do that defining for me. I wanted people to talk about how I projected kindness and love while showing strength and determination when they think of my brand and me. Don't get me wrong; talking about your athletic career will always send you over the hump in different conversations, but it's not your definition.

Always giving a friendly smile and speaking to everyone that I crossed paths with showed me these things. Offering to help others before they ask for your help can go a long way. Always keep your intentions genuine and be a man or woman of your word. If you say that you are going to do something, do it! Your approach and delivery to how you work and your ability to execute a plan will speak volumes in your defense. You won't need many words because your actions are proven evidence that you follow through.

Building your identity does not have to happen when you are no longer active in your sport. It starts the moment that you decide who you are and who you want to become. Always stay true to your values, morals, and be real. Never forget where you started. Growth is essential, and change is still bound to happen. As long as you are changing for the better, don't ever let anyone make you feel guilty for wanting to invest in your identity.

As I have gotten older, I started to feel that no one knows what they want to do for the rest of their lives. With growth, change happens. That is just my opinion. The rest of their lives could be a very long time or a short time, as living tomorrow is not promised. Enjoy your life. Finding purpose is more fulfilling than planning a successful life. Success will come to you, but you will always find yourself looking for your next success if you live like this. My advice is to find purpose in what you do, even if that's in bursts of life.

Things change a lot, especially in life. As human beings, we can love what we do. That feeling can sustain us. Sometimes circumstances can change or end that will be out of your control. With uncontrollable situations, knowing who you are will need to be your priority. Your identity scavenger hunt is more about what the world can NOT take from you. Don't misinterpret this; the dreamers should always dream. I would never sway anyone away from their heart's desire.

Our treasures on Earth comes from what's inside of our hearts. It's only right to fulfill and pursue those dreams. The blurred lines follow those who do not have an action plan. You can do anything you want in this life. Having a plan and knowing who you are is equally important.

What Are Your Natural Talents?

While playing sports can be demanding, especially in college, keep your perspective open to learning new things. What you gain can show you different things that you are good at or things that you can use in the future. In high school, I can remember focusing so hard on basketball that I did not even care to play another sport or consider other hobbies. I was afraid that it would take me away from basketball. It's not a big problem, but high school should be a time of exploring and expanding creativity. This part is where creativity originates before you begin to explore how big the world is. Your creativity is limitless.

Naturally, things that come to you are the life gifts you were given and trusted to possess. Knowing your natural talents will carry you through life. Just like your sport, before you began playing, it was natural for you. For instance, when I first picked up a basketball, I started dribbling and doing layups. It did not feel awkward. I did not struggle to learn the basic mechanic or coordination for those skills until my game needed to advance. Things are always more natural before it turns into an IQ and instinct game. I was naturally fit for the game.

You may have had the same situation by playing sports. You just had the natural ability and talent. When the levels advanced, you started breaking down the fundamentals and other aspects of your sports training. It's inevitable that the higher the scale, the better the competition. You have to make sure you are up to par with your skills.

Writing and the art of storytelling or poetry was natural for me, outside of basketball. My prayer is that as you read this book that you leave feeling inspired and know that you are not alone. I want every reader to see that you are somebody outside of sports, and that comes from searching within. I'm not sure, exactly, what my life purpose is, but I do believe that our mission is what is already within us and inside of our hearts. At this moment, my purpose was to create T.O.O.L's Beyond Sports.

My spirit kept me isolated and feeling alone, many times, while in pursuit of playing. I had to take ownership of my life and understand that I was getting near the end of my playing career. There's no one to blame as you can alter the narrative in your story. It was during the times that the game was on pause for me that made me remember that it will end. This book is not just for me but for all of us.

You might be an excellent writer as well. I never claimed to be perfect or an author. I'm utilizing my natural gift to get my message across. My goal is to speak to as many people as I can, through this book, and inspire you to believe that life does not end when our playing days are over. Everyone goes through an array of emotions that comes with transitioning, especially athletes, especially if that is all we have identified with for a decade or more.

We do not realize that we are on an identity scavenger hunt when trying to decide and figure out what is coming next. I do not have all of the answers, but I am confident that when you make peace with your journey and who you are, that will make the transition smoother.

While in college, I knew athletes who majored in sports-related fields. Because I was good at writing, I originally majored in Communication with an emphasis in journalism. My high school was a school of Communication. It is something about how broad and diverse the field is that made me choose that route. The art of communications grew on me because I was able to be creative in many areas: writing, videography, photography, radio, television, and film, to name a few.

Later, I changed my major to Corporate Communication because the university that I attended only had that option. I figured that I could use it somewhere, one day. I am not saying that school is the only resource to get where you want to go. For me, it was basketball that opened my mind to college. Studying in such a creative degree plan allowed me to create outside of basketball. Creativity breeds self-discovery.

While I had teammates that were struggling with mathematics and definition terminology on tests, my assignments were literally to create. I've had the opportunity to produce digital communication, magazines, training & development programs, and film projects. These projects were not easy. I was having fun, learning, and increasing my identity capital without realizing it. I am not endorsing a particular degree program or field. I am suggesting that you study something that will keep you versatile, keep you happy, gives you freedom, and supports you to live the life you choose. You want to have the same fun and passion with everything you enjoy because true happiness begins and ends from the inside.

Don't be the person who does something because it's popular or trending. That will lead you down an unfulfilled road. Jumping from one thing to the next is exhausting and not valid to who you are. You have to do what makes you happy. Try new things. You have the right to like or dislike something. You also have the right to change your mind about what you thought you wanted. Don't let the world or money influence or discourage who you are and what you thoroughly enjoy. Rely on what comes natural and accessible to you.

They say that you become the people you hang with and the things that you do. You might have seasons of hibernation and seasons of celebration. There will be people you outgrow on your journey. Don't take this personal. Don't try to force things to work. Let things happen naturally. Eventually, things work themselves out. In your identity scavenger hunt, you should always be growing. Never let anyone take you back to a level that you departed. Your growth is a personal investment: treat it as such.

For the athletes who have the opportunity to visit another country to play, try to learn their language. Not just for the basics but open yourself up to it if you're interested in full conversation. Most athletes that play internationally will spend from 3 to 12 months away, depending on the market and the length of their season. How many people do you know who are bi-lingual? If you are in another state, learn the culture and history of the areas you roam every day. You have to be open-minded and intentional about trying new things.

Leveraging opportunities to learn for free is when you will realize how present you are. The only person who can hold you back is yourself. Always be confident in your approach and have a real genuine spirit. Do not try to take advantage of something free with expectations of entitlement or an ungrateful heart.

If you know that you want to be a coach one day, why not start while playing? You have direct access to your current coaches. See if it's possible to shadow them. Sit in on their meetings if you have the opportunity. Learn how the recruiting process works from a coach's perspective. It won't hurt to ask. I learned that a closed mouth wouldn't get fed. If you are a former athlete and always wanted to do sports reporting, how about setting up a meeting with reporters who worked your games?

Take advantage of opportunities when they are available. Find ways to create opportunities that are not available. To discover new things about yourself and discover new talents, you will have to do something that you usually don't do. Sometimes these discoveries happen by accident. Face your fears and challenge yourself. You never know what will happen.

Time Out

Knowing the difference between what you do and who you are is critical. Rewire your thinking and rebuild your identity. Sports will always be a part of who you are but just a piece.

Take Action

- Reflect on who you are.
- What does your identity mean to you?
- What do you like outside of sports?
- What are five characteristics that make you who you are?

PRE-SEASON CONDITIONING
"Preparing for Opportunities"

3

"When you want to succeed as bad as you want to breathe, then you'll be successful."

-ERIC THOMAS

(Thomas, 2011).

As athletes, we know that being prepared takes commitment, discipline, practice, and a high level of focus. Preparation in conditioning season is for your mind and body to perform. It's your consistency that gives you the ultimate confidence that you are ready. When we are younger, we think that the more we work on our physical skills, the better of an athlete we will become. Although it's real and you must work on your skills to get better, it begins to turn into a mental game. As we develop, preparation is more about patience and discipline. When we get older or mature in the game, we realize that training will not always be physical.

Preparation begins to turn into watching your diet and nutrition. Diet and nutrition help with sports performance and endurance to sustain your position for a complete season. Film study is another factor in preparing. Film study helps you prepare for your opponent and learn their habits in an attempt to stop their plans. Studying film also shows where you made a mistake and where you can make adjustments, within a play, in your next game.

A factor in preparation is proper rest and recovery. Sometimes sacrifices have to be made to be prepared. These are a few examples, outside of skill development, that require preparation. You have to have the same mindset as you prepare for other opportunities in life after sports.

When we hear our coaches say the word "conditioning," we automatically connect it with physical exhaustion. In some instances, we mentally defeat ourselves because we know what we are against when the coach says that word. I can remember always reminding myself that running sprints, in pre-season basketball conditioning, were only 10-15 second bursts at a time. The faster I run, the more time I could recover during each break to catch my breath. I was always one of the fastest or the fastest player on my teams. That's not a bragging right. It's the truth.

Deep down, conditioning was always my least favorite part of the process. Looking at me and the way I trained my mind, you could never tell that I didn't like it. The type of player I was, I had to give 110%

effort in conditioning. I relied heavily on my speed and quickness, so I took my sprint conditioning seriously. Either I'm going to be tired or my opponent. The way I looked at it is that speed was one of my strengths, so I needed that to work in my full advantage every single practice and game.

The bottom line is that conditioning starts with YOU. It starts with accountability. Your coach can only prepare you as best as possible, but it must be up to you to get the maximum out of the preparation. Conditioning requires effort! Only you will know if you have been preparing or if you have been lacking. When it's time to perform, the truth will show. You know what it takes to train for practice and games. You won't see football players, conditioning like soccer players. You won't see softball players conditioning like basketball players. For one, it's not necessary. For two, each sport requires a different type of conditioning.

As you begin to immerse yourself in your transition after sports, keep in mind that you have the tools you need. All you need to do is condition yourself for your opportunities. It's the same approach but a different game. You may not have to condition yourself as you do as an athlete, but you will need to prepare yourself for opportunities. One of my favorite tools is preparing yourself for opportunities because of the challenges that you have at war. It will make or break you. That battle is only between where you are and where you want to be.

Know Your Position & Know Your Role

Before pre-season, you sharpen your skills and work on individual goals in the off-season. Your commitment begins before returning to your team or joining your team. The off-season is where you have time to reflect on what went well, what did not go well, and what can help you become a better version of yourself for the upcoming season. If you enter pre-season out of shape, your coaches will see your commitment level, and you have to work twice as hard during pre-season conditioning. Your coaches prepare a pre-season plan based on their philosophy, the team's identity, and how far they think they can push each person individually.

During the pre-season, you get a glimpse of who you will be working with, playing with you, and learning everything in the operation of who you are. Some of your pre-season teammates won't be your regular-season teammates. Some teammates may not make it to playoffs.

People fall off for personal reasons, injuries, or they just happen to go in other directions. We see this all of the time in sports. It's no secret. Staying committed to your goals individually will help you filter your way through, no matter what circumstances happen. Never think about giving up on yourself, no matter how the dice rolls.

Before you arrived at your team, you may have played a different position with another team. Your playing position may have changed from high school to college to professional. Your role could vary from season to season or day-to-day. When there is a plethora of talent, or lack of, surrounding you, all you need to do is play your role, and do it well, to achieve the team's success.

In basketball, while there are point guards who facilitate and lead the floor well, there are also point guards that are on a team where they have to score first so that their teammates can follow suit. Spectators will judge and say that the first point guard should score more or the other should pass more. On the outside looking in, people will always have opinions and speculations. In sports, you know that you have to remain flexible. Your ability to adapt to change, game to game, may increase a greater responsibility in your leadership on your team. What does not change is your position within that team.

You could be a player that was known for coming off of the bench. When it's your time to play, you know that you have to bring a different energy into the game. You have to stay consistent in your role. At whatever point, your coach has put you into the game based on what the team needs and what you bring to the game. It took me a long time to understand this: You are always valuable, no matter what the situation is. Coming off the bench is just as important as a starting position.

During my sophomore year in college, my coach decided to make an example out of me. It was all respect, but she wanted to show the team that you are not entitled because you are leading from the front. She noticed that I started to get comfortable in my role, even when I underperformed. She decided to take me out of the starting line up in a game that we should have lost. In hindsight, maybe she was doing this to challenge me differently.

Well, I came into the game with a different attitude, and not once did I complain. I played my role, with a chip on my shoulder, to prove why I was a leader on that team. We were down the whole time. The game came down to the last 30 seconds. I cashed out to win the game at the free-throw line. She ruffled my feathers a bit, but she also knew the value that I brought to our team. I did not start the game, but she could not deny me of finishing the game for the victory. Hard work will always prevail.

The moral of that story is that although she took me out of the starting lineup for one game, that did not change my position, it just altered my role. No matter what part you play, you have to make it happen. You have to know that there will be some things out of your control. There will be people in positions that can move you around, but you have to know who you are and what your job is within that organization. If you fall into the trap of feeling sorry for yourself or think that the world is against you, you will crumble.

It's easy to get comfortable once we adapt to new environments and situations but always think before you react. There will be obstacles to test you, who you are, and what you thought you knew. Think before you act. How you respond to adversity will always set you apart.

Creating value should always be at the forefront of your list. No matter what role you have to play, think of ways to create value in your position. Start with knowing yourself, stay true to who you are, and believing in your abilities. Never be afraid or back down from any challenge. People challenge you to see what your response will be. While they wait for your answer, don't react. Show up with grace and win in style. Not only are they watching, but everyone around you is watching as well.

In business or a career path, the position that you want will require a little research. Don't just apply for a job or sign up for a role because it pays well or because of the company name. Sometimes the research study will include you looking into the history and getting a feel for the culture. Sometimes, the research will allow you to volunteer for the organization and learn as much as you can. It's better to embrace a role that you like and could grow to love instead of something that is forced from you or on you. Read that again.

In any position you are in, you want to know what's connected. Always know who will manage you, see the business, see the CEO, the president, etc. These are the people that you will need to know and who others will speak of in conversation in your industry. Be informed on what's going on in your business or career field. Staying informed always keeps you ahead of the game. Study the greats and gain experience if you decide to launch your own business. Make the mistakes as you continue to learn.

Professionalism

In sports, it's the small things that coaches and scouts look for outside of talent. Sportsmanship, attitude, and punctuality are just a few. Small actions make a significant difference and are far from insignificant. The great thing about these qualities and characteristics is that you can determine and control it. What cannot be controlled is someone portraying these characteristics for you.

Professionalism is a real thing. The way that you carry yourself will always be people's perception of you. People will never forget the details they see on you that make a big difference because it's easy for humans to judge humans. I'm not saying you have to be a specific way to impress others. I'm just saying that you should always be your most authentic self and be professional at the same time. If you don't remember anything else in this chapter, remember this:

YOU NEVER KNOW WHO IS WATCHING YOU!

Your appearance and presentation are EVERYTHING. You do not have to have the most money in the room to keep yourself intact. It's something about the way that you look that correlates to your mood and how you feel. My best days are when I take my time preparing with wardrobe, hair, necessities, and other grooming. I am a firm believer in wearing the clothes that make you feel your best and always top it off with a smile!

Your appearance is a gold mine. Your approach is your gateway. You are your brand and what you represent before you introduce yourself. I did not say that you need to have the top designer in your wardrobe, especially if you can't afford it. Wearing what makes you feel comfortable and confident will make it natural. The best advice I received in the professional world was to treat every day like an interview or possible business exchange. First impressions are how people remember you. You never know if it is someone's first time noticing you.

In life after sports, the preparations that you face will be mental. What you make a priority will determine the time that you put into it. What you make a priority will be a commitment. See it through. You know that whatever you set your mind to do, you will achieve. You will overcome any obstacles on your path because it lives inside of your athletic DNA.

Time Out

Sometimes you just have to try new things and trust that your journey is for you to excel. Maximize the opportunities that you hold. Sometimes you will think that you are not ready for opportunities because of fear. Do it afraid and grow. You have to recognize every opportunity that you have. It starts with you. Keep yourself in position.

Take Action

- Reflect on your best year of pre-season conditioning.
- How did you prepare for your season?
- What did you learn about yourself and the position that you were preparing for?
- How will you prepare for your next opportunity?

2nd Quarter

Get Your Momentum Going

RESPECT THE GAME
"Always Respect Yourself, Your Opponent, Your Position"

4

"You are never really playing an opponent. You are playing yourself, your own highest standards, and when you reach your limits, that is real joy."

-ARTHUR ASHE

(Walker, 2015).

Respect Yourself

What do you feed yourself? Not physically, in terms of food, but in your everyday affirmations. Affirmations are positive notes to yourself. One thing I learned is self-respect and how to talk to myself. You have to be your number one supporter in life, believe in yourself, and believe in your abilities. Some people will talk themselves out of opportunities and moments of excellence because of how they are conditioned to speak to themselves.

Instead of asking yourself: Why is this not working?

Tell yourself: I will figure out different ways to make this work.

The more you tell yourself that you can't or don't know how to do something will lead to a negative result. Fixing your thought pattern is respecting yourself. You have to be able to respect yourself before you can respect your opponent or respect your position. This is you holding accountability for yourself in your hands. How do you treat yourself? How do you talk to yourself? Be gentle with yourself and know when you need to be hard on yourself. Whenever you give your absolute best at whatever you set out to do, do not kick yourself in your knee.

I remember when I used to get frustrated at myself for missing free-throws as if I am a perfect human being. I would have poor body language and curse at myself as if it were the end of the world. Although I thought this was motivating me, and it was, that did not stop the fact that I had not shown myself any respect and that the response to me was negative.

I did not realize that I was being so mean to myself because it was like I had normalized talking bad to myself. Instead of giving myself positive affirmations and taking a deep breath, I was negatively responding to myself. My intentions were for the best, but my response was not showing that. My body language and demeanor eventually followed an adverse reaction because of how I was talking to myself. We have to be careful with the way we talk to ourselves because it will be a direct response to our whole being, which may not transfer positively.

When you respect yourself, you take care of yourself and understand that you have to do what keeps you feeling your best if you want to present your best self. Self-care is one of the most under-rated essential needs of life. If you are not any good for yourself, what good can you be to anyone else or for anything you want to give your best effort?

In the professional world, I hear many people talking and asking about work/life balance. Work/life balance is essential to self-care. Being a natural-born go-getter, hustler, or how you wish to define your "means to get it" is a high mentality. Sometimes, though, we have to stop and know when we are neglecting ourselves in the process.

Overworking can cause burn out. Burn out is no joke. If you have ever done a set of push-ups, in continuous motion, imagine an overworking burn out is similar to this. When you do burn out push-ups, you are not supposed to stop until your arms give out. Your upper body will just collapse.

Overworking, in reality, turns into being overwhelmed mentally, physically, and emotionally. While we must work and execute our goals, we must also take care of ourselves. Finding things that bring you balance takes away from the everyday stresses of life and work. I experienced burn out before and did not know when to stop until I was forced to. You have to make time to relax and wind down.

Making time to relax is like recovery day from practices and games. If you do not have that following day off from a game, coaches know the result will not be positive. Recovery is necessary to get the treatment for healing that your body needs to be able to perform. It's the same thing in life after athletics. Therapy for me could be as simple as doing yoga, a nail salon visit, or doing absolutely nothing. You have to find what works for you and create your own balance so that you can operate at your best, for yourself, those you love, and for what you love.

Don't get so caught up in trying to make a living that you forget to live your life. One of my best friends repeats that to me often. It does not mean that I'm not living my life. It just means that sometimes we can put so much focus on one area that we start to neglect other areas in life. Self-care is essential to your well-being. Don't feel bad or feel like you are missing out on anything when you take one day off from everything.

Respect Your Opponent

It does not matter which way the ball bounces, your current opponent has something in common with you. You are on the same level and have endured some of the same things to be able to stand where you are in the moment. Their journey may not have been like your journey, but both of your adventures led you to stand side by side. When you look at your opponent, respect him/her/it. Your opponent may not always be a person. Your opponent could be an obstacle in your way.

Respect should always be the end result of facing opposition. If your opponent is adversity, use the opportunity to grow. The opposition will have you questioning yourself, your value, and what you believe in. When this happens, stay true to who you are and always stand firm in what you believe in while allowing yourself to grow. What you face serves a purpose. Being open-minded and respecting the situation will propel you.

You want to make the best of opportunities to learn about yourself, your opponent, and the situation. Experience is the best teacher because no one can tell you how you will respond in any case. Similar oppositions will always resurface until you learn from personal experience and how to handle it, each time it occurs.

Imagine your team has a rival with an organization. In the past three years, your record is 1-2, meaning you won 1 and lost 2 games or competitions. You feel that you will gain more respect when you break even so you will treat the next match as a must-win. You have enough respect for your opponent to have a game plan in motion, and you have prepared yourself as best as you can to leave the competition with a victory. From past experiences, you approach the opposition with respect, knowing what the journey has been for the past three years when facing this opponent.

When you win, make sure you win with grace. You respect the opponent, and in turn, the opponent respects you. Even if they don't respect you, both parties understand the journey of what it takes to get the victory and what you have to go through to get on the other side of defeat. You may not always win, immediately, but you will when you learn to respect your opponent.

Respect Your Position

You are qualified for any position you earn. You know what it took to earn a spot on your team. It keeps you humbled, knowing that you are not entitled. Having a work ethic is what you will need to get the position, maintain the job, and grow from the situation. Use the position you are in, don't let it use you. Let your position serve a purpose bigger than yourself.

Please do not confuse the position with the working title. Your work title is just that: A title, a description of your role within the job itself. As you grow and understand your position, you will walk in gratitude. When people approach you to learn about your journey and how you got to where you are, they're looking at the position. Let your journey inspire, mentor, and encourage the next generation. Believe it or not, you may be an inspiration to those around you.

When you maximize the opportunities of where you are, you will inevitably produce fruit. Producing fruit from a healthy tree is essential. Picture yourself as that tree. Do you want to create or influence the strawberries that are fresh and juicy, or do you want to be the strawberry that caused the other berries to mold because it sat in the fridge too long and molded? If you water your garden, the seeds will grow. Maximizing the position and opportunity that you are in is an everyday job.

Never look down on others on your way up. When you see and feel someone leaning on you, help them up. Don't be insecure or fear that they will outshine you. Be secure in your position and know that when the people that are connected to you win, you win as well. Remember where you came from and never lose sight of the work you put in to grow and be in the position that you are in.

There may come a time when the people who helped you on your way up, lean on you as well. We all need each other. Be inspired when people look up to you for hope, inspiration, and direction through example. It's not about helping to attain something worldly but helping others be the best versions of themselves so that they can maximize where they are and grow into a person in a unique position.

Life is a journey, so do not bite the hand that feeds you because you can be up, and you can be down. When you respect where you are, the people that helped you, the people you helped, and the position that you are in, everything connected to you will grow. Refresh your perspective and stay in position. There are lives connected to your growth as your life may be connected to their growth.

Time Out

You can only give what you have inside. Be careful how you treat yourself because it will reflect in the way you treat others. Respect is a principle that can really affect everything and every person around you.

Take Action

- Reflect on how you treat yourself.
- How do you talk to yourself?
- What are two ways that you could better treat yourself?
- How do you show respect to others?
- In what ways do you respect your position?

CREATE A TEAM

"Networking"

5

"Believe in yourself and there will come a day when others will have no choice but to believe with you."

-MUFASA

(The Lion King Movie, 2019).

Building your network requires you to do an individual assessment of what you need. Networking is about more than what someone can do for you. The value should be exchanged from both parties. Your network will not always be the people that you are surrounded by every day. You should be pleased with the culture you build within your network, regardless of how it's put together.

Creating your team (network) will require you to connect with people who are moving in the same direction as you are in life. It does not mean that you have to be in the same field doing the same kind of work. It just means that like attracts like, so let it develop organically.

When we join a team, we enter a culture. When we create a team, we create a culture. Defining what the culture will be is up to you. Keep in mind that whatever you dish out is what you will get in return. Your approach in defining your culture should be measured in quality. Many people think that quantity is more important, but it is not. Build a quality network. Character, attitude, work ethic, trustworthiness, etc. are a few qualities that will always outnumber a group of people who lack morals and ethics.

Every team, or individual, in sports or their workplace, build their culture based on mission statements and team mantras. Every year, a team may adopt a new mantra, but their organization's mission statement is the foundation, so it stays the same. The team players change, year to year. The organization is set in place. A mission statement is the organization's "why." It's the purpose behind its' existence. A mantra is a group of words, or phrases, that are lived by for motivational and encouragement purposes. This could be what the current coach implements. The culture is built around individuals who believe in the same principles and have the same attitude toward achieving the organization's goal while sharing its vision. Follow me as we create your team through this written context.

Be Your Own General Manager

I love how, in sports, general managers know what they are lacking by mid-season and in the off-season. Before things get out of control, they are aware of potential players that could add value to their roster and those who do not fit with their team. Sometimes business decisions have to be made. You are the general manager of your team and those that surround you. It is not always easy, but necessary adjustments must be made for your personal life and professional growth.

Diversifying your personnel and being open to pieces that could provide a boost and value to your environment could be the game-changer that you need. In my profession, I try not to limit myself to only communicating with the people that I work with directly. Meeting new people and learning about their position, roles, and life journeys always spark my interest. You would be surprised at how much you may have in common with someone you are completely different from.

You don't have to limit your team to what you are familiar with. Sometimes you need a presence that you just do not understand but seems to always make a difference. As long as you have a genuine approach and plan, you can add value to your team. The primary key is to know who is on your side and what value is being exchanged. If at any time, you feel devalued or feel a piece losing value, you have to make adjustments if you want to progress. I'm not saying to cut people off, but maybe you limit their playing time and stay connected as a role player. Create those boundaries.

Mentors

In sports, our first line of networking typically comes in the form of a coach or trainer. Think about the one coach or coaches who made a difference in your life. Although you were an addition to their team, you don't realize it but, you made them a part of your team.

If your coach helped with your athletic and personal development, they became a mentor for you. Mentors can be essential because you can always seek advice or guidance, whether you ask for it or not. Sometimes the information is sports related. Other times it's related to life. The way you evaluate and apply the advice will display in your level of concern for that matter. Their job is not to tell you what to do or what's best for you but to guide you in making the best decisions.

A coach is not only a person who teaches in sports. There are many coaches in the world. You could have a business, financial, and wellness coach. They all have one thing in common. They all teach based on a subject matter. If you did not have a coach who became a mentor for you, maybe you looked up to a great coach in the virtual world. You sought out what qualities you thought made this coach great, in your eyes.

Virtual mentors are just as important as the ones who are present. These are the people that you relate to through online interviews and follow them for different perspectives to help you navigate in your world. The next time you go online, search your favorite person to listen to. Remember, they may not be physically present, but you always have access to them, virtually.

Take Accountability

Everyone has a goal to win. When you create a team, make sure that your goals are clear. The outcome of your goals will not always be to help you gain a position or some type of status. When you create a reliable team that you can learn from, and they can learn from you, value is created. Know that you might not win, right away, every time you set a goal, but don't blame the pieces that YOU put together. Take a look at yourself. Always take accountability and figure out how you can get better and continue to evolve.

As early as elementary days, we tend to separate ourselves and create our own societies, in the form of friends. Don't limit yourself as you grow, though. Shake up your world every now and then. Always be kind to others. Not because you want something but because it becomes a part of who you are. It's best to begin peer networking as early as high school, through college, and early in your profession. One day you will realize how it's funny that we reconnect with the people that we rarely talked with while in high school and college.

Your teachers, parents, coaches, mentors, business partners, etc. are not responsible for achieving your goals. They can only support you and hold their own weight. If you feel that you are not getting that support, always remember not to put any expectations on any person or situation, except for yourself. You are the general manager of the team and the world that you create. The only thing you can control is you and your response to situations that you are involved in.

Time Out

Be your own general manager and create your team. Know the kind of culture, staff, and players you want when it's time for you to battle in the game of life. Who can you learn from?

Take Action

- Reflect on what makes a great team.
- What qualities do you look for in a teammate?
- What makes you a good teammate?
- How do you take accountability when you and your team are not performing?

GET IN THE GAME

"Resources are Key"

6

"Ultimately, life is about value exchange. Give value to get value."

-GARY VAYNERCHUK

(Vaynerchuk, 2016).

When you get in the game, you know that being aggressive gives you momentum. If you were a starter on your team, you built enough trust in the teammates that you start with. They rely on you as that leader to get the team going. If you were inserted into the game rotation, you know that you are just as valuable because you can shift the energy of the game and give your team the boost needed at any given time. Starter or role player, you needed one another for the common goal of winning games. You did not handpick your teammates in organized sports, your coaches did. If you picked your teammates, it was in a regular pick-up game or by creating your team, like in the previous chapter.

In any situation, you were able to learn your team. The longer you play with your teammates, the more you pick up on what gives them confidence or what is less comfortable. For a basketball player, you learned what kind of passes your teammates needed to complete a play, get a good shot, or simply catch the ball. A quarterback, in football, knows what receivers are capable of capturing the Hail Mary passes in the end zone. A volleyball player knows how to set a volleyball, at the right angle, for their teammate. A relay runner knows where to place the baton for their teammate.

In all situations, you knew your team's personnel and what your teammates needed because of spending several hours of practice together. You made it work because your teammates were your resources, as you were to them, to achieve your common team goals. You knew what worked for everyone else, but did you ever evaluate what actually worked for you?

Resources are crucial when you are moving through life. Knowing how to use your resources can separate where you are to where you are trying to go. It's all about building your relationships, knowing who surrounds you, and knowing when to move forward. It's like having a scouting report. Before you get into the game, you have to know your personnel and the position of each person that you are affiliated with and know which direction you are going. In this case, the best assessment is to know yourself, what you can contribute, and how you can make your teammates better. Orchestrate your offense and get in the game!

How Are Your Relationships?

For other relationships to flourish, the one with yourself has to be in order. When you get into the game, you have to be motivated. You can't give what you don't possess. You can only give what you have inside. Having relationships with like-minded individuals connects you with shared interests, ideas, and perspectives. These qualities should also be challenged. Do not be a yes man because something sounds good. Think about the ideas and perspectives that people share with you. Form your own opinion and respect the thoughts of both parties. Everything that surrounds you is a mirror into yourself. How you treat yourself is how you will set the standard of how you choose to be treated. Life is a reflection!

Who Surrounds You?

If your only friends are athletes, we have a problem. If all of your friends are people that you grew up with, we have a problem. If your only friends are the people that are within your everyday life, we have a problem. You do not need to befriend every person you meet but always grow your network. I'm not taking away from the relationships that you currently hold, but I want you to continually add growth in your inner circle and surroundings. The relationships you now have may or may not be available for what you need next on your journey.

I just want you to recognize that and remind you to always keep yourself in a position to grow. When you are in the game and know your personnel, you go on a progressive run to eventually put yourself in a position to win. No one is discredited for contribution to the game. Every possession was needed to get to victory. Efficiency and consistency are where trust is built from moments of adversity and good times.

Some friends may have to get fewer minutes of playing time, depending on your current situation (the game). You may have to rely heavily on others, at times. Make sure that you are not using people for what they can do for you but for what you can do for them. Keep it real.

When the roles are reversed, and they have to rely on you, make yourself available in value. As long as there is value exchanged, time and position do not matter.

For a long time, the majority of my surroundings were either athletes or people of my age. That is no problem. However, that could have also limited my thinking and my world. I'm not taking away from any of these relationships. Life just started to become more interesting when I opened my horizon to people from all walks of life.

There are times when I depend on my vets (the OG's, the seasoned, however you want to label them) because I'm younger. My vets are the people that I consider friends that are seasoned or older than me with experience. I currently have five vets that I learn from and apply life lessons to my personal life. All five of these vets range from my mothers' age to beyond my grandmother's age. I have friends that are my age, but my vets are the ones that give me the wisdom, beyond the years that I have lived, that I can't get from the friends that are my age. When I feel lost or stagnant, I know that I can get advice on some of their experiences that will progress where I am in the game.

Study the Game

To play in the game, you have to work on the fundamentals daily. To be really good, you have to work on your skills and find ways to set you apart. I think that being distinguished in the game requires studying the game. Learning means being abreast, knowing what is going on at all times, and being able to insert yourself like a pro.

Watching the game as a fan is for fun and entertainment. Studying the game is for the ones who want to be a part of something bigger than themselves. Don't get so caught up in watching the game that you forget to put yourself in and contribute to your own progress. In whatever you decide to do after sports, remember that the same game is being played and no one is going to give you something because of who you are. The more you grow, the more adversity will try to bring you down. All in all, you will continue to get better.

The best thing about studying is that it is a choice. If you choose to study, you increase your curiosity and creativity. Knowing a business before you get in that game will help you learn how things operate and the patterns of the brand/business success within an industry. Look and see who holds the status to sit high in command. Sometimes you just need to look in your space and study the ones who are winners. When you study success, their patterns can help you innovate and create your own success. Do your homework! Why accept barely passing through the back door when you can be trusted to lead the front of the class?

Are You Involved?

Most of us are introduced to clubs (music, sports, karate, drama, chess, etc.), in grade school. If we join those clubs, it's usually because our friends pull us along or we pull them along. In middle school, we start figuring out if we actually like opportunities or consider them lame because we want to be so cool. In high school, we start looking for our identity through our friendships and what we like. If we are focused, we start zoning in on what we are actually good at. In college, we disregard anything that is not class-related or hinders our life as student-athletes.

Well, all of those opportunities were prime years to know what it was like to really be involved in something other than sports. It's harder to make time for other avenues when one thing demands most of your time. This is where the work and life balance will start to kick in.

You are not alone if you missed the opportunity to be involved in other high school or college activities. Guess what? Life is not over, and you still have time. You can join clubs/organizations that you are interested in. You would be surprised at how much being a part of an organization could change your life/career/business. The people that you meet may have the potential to be lifetime connections.

When I joined my first organization, I was just a member. I wanted to go and network and meet as many people as I could. I did not really have a goal other than seeking opportunities. When I put myself in the game, I did not want to be average anymore, so I found ways to immerse myself in joining a committee within the organization. That is a game-changer when you are really involved in professional organizations. This is the time to communicate with executives, learn from them, and learn new things during your process to help create an organizational impact or help your own business flourish.

The Internet

Anything you want to learn is connected to your hands and fingers. Technology is advanced with unlimited resources and connections. There is almost no excuse as to why you should not be aware of or know how to find something. All of this is practically free.

There was a time before the 2000s when people had to sit in libraries and hope to discover books that gave them the necessary information. It's almost scary that now people forget that libraries exist and have the same resources and more on a better scale. In fact, I have used about 50 percent of writing this book, inside of study rooms in the local libraries. Everything in the library is free. Searching for something on the internet is free.

One year, in college, I did not have a cell phone. I pretty much finessed the system with communication. I bought an iPod when the touch screen versions were released. Wi-Fi was becoming popular, and literally, every place existing were starting to install Wi-Fi for customers. Well, I downloaded a free app that allowed free texting and phone calls. This app gave me a regular phone number, which is how I communicated for one year without a phone bill. If I could still do it today, I would. The only reason I can't is that most Wi-Fi can only be accessed when you're in its presence. I'm also not that college student that really has no need for a phone as much as I need one now.

The moral of this story is that you can't make excuses for why something cannot work when you are in the game. There are plenty of options, you just have to be creative and find ways to make things work.

You can't have one foot out and one foot in the game. Either you are all in, or you will be left behind. Either you want to play the game or watch the game from the stands. You have the option to make things work for you or to make excuses. Look at what you have. Look at your resources. I don't think people realize how creative they are when they make excuses. If you can think of one million ways why something can't work but can't think of two ways why that same thing can work, then you need to readjust your thinking and search within.

Time Out

Sitting on the sidelines as a spectator is easy. Spectators can form opinions on what everyone should do from a different view. It's a different ball game when you are actually in the game. Block out the people in the stands and stick to your script.

Take Action

- Reflect on how you mentally prepare to get in the game.
- What can you study for your next chapter in life?
- Are you a student of life and of your path?
- What can you be involved in that helps you keep the sports element added to your life?

Half

Time

Photography from Jack Yates High School Class of 2010 Senior Yearbook).

PATRINA GOREE #22

A lot of hard work and conditioning took place in this gym and with this team. We had one common goal and that was to win!

(Photography from Jack Yates High School Class of 2010 Senior Yearbook).

Eastern Oklahoma State College in Wilburton Oklahoma, (2011-2012).

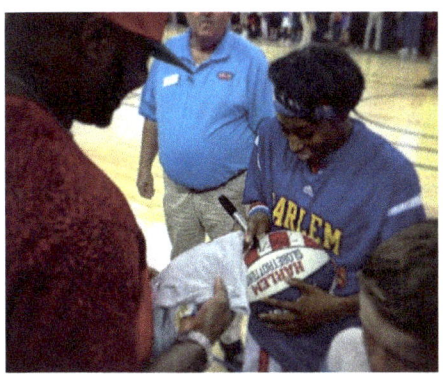

PATRINA GOREE with her sister's father after a Harlem Globetrotters game, (2016).

Thank you, Gary, for your support and watching me play basketball on every level.

LMBPF League in Mexico City, Mexico.
Team: Quetzales Sajoma Club, (2017).

PATRINA GOREE at WISE Houston Speed Mentoring Roundtable, (2019).

PATRINA GOREE (TRINA) visits the National Junior College Athletic Association National Office, (2020).

3rd Quarter

Follow Through

GET ON OFFENSE

"Drive Your Vehicle, Find Your Lanes"

7

"I've always felt it was not up to anyone else to make me give my best."

-HAKEEM OLAJUWON

(IBD Staff, 2016).

After reflecting on your journey with an identity scavenger hunt, you have put yourself in a position to prepare for opportunities by creating your team and putting yourself in the game. The game of life after sports. As long as you have breath in your body, you can find your lane to operate in your purpose in this life. When you are on offense, this means that the ball is in your possession. The objective is obviously to have a plan or strategize on ways that you can defeat obstacles that arise, in the game, so that you can win.

Great players know that good offense comes from having superior defensive possessions. In this chapter, my goal is to help you drive your vehicle with an offensive mindset. In an actual vehicle, I was told, to drive my car for the other people on the road and give myself a chance to make it to my destination safely. This leaves you paying attention to everyone else around you to make sure you can stay safe. If I carried this mindset in life, it would leave me paying attention to everyone and what they have going on around me, instead of what's in my lane and where I wanted to go.

In life, I chose to do the opposite and take risks to achieve the goals I set for myself. I do not focus on anybody else's lane except my own. I'm aware of what's going on around me, but I am solely focused on what I need to do to get to where I am going in my vehicle. I don't want to lose sight of myself and miss my exit, miss my turning point, or miss when it's time to go into another direction, so I focus on my mission.

Waiting on someone to make moves on my behalf is playing timid, in my opinion. It's defensive. I don't want to wait to see what someone is going to do, on my behalf, so that I can make a move. In my playing career, I got tired of waiting on others for responses or direction on where I had my vision and started playing offense. It's no one's responsibility to play the game for you, so you can't expect them to score when you want them to.

Every once in a while, or however often you need to, it's okay to pull your vehicle over and check to make sure that it is in good condition to keep going. You have the keys to your vehicle. It's okay for you to make a pit stop. Stop to cry, grieve, repair, and restore so that you can keep moving toward your destination. Just don't prolong your stop. Get back on the road until you make it to where you want to go.

With your vehicle, you take it for maintenance when it needs an oil change or when service lights appear. If you make it for service maintenance in a timely fashion, you usually get the problem resolved as soon as possible, depending on how urgent the service is needed. The support of your vehicle ensures that it is secure on the roads. When you take care of your car, it continues to get you from destination to destination.

When you really want something in your life, sometimes the only person blocking you is yourself. Adjust your mirror and look deeper into yourself. If you are not where you want to be, I want you to take ownership of that and stop blaming the cards you were dealt with and situations that came your way to tear you down. With all of the obstacles that come from negative forces, the last thing you need is to be in your own way. There is no need to continually look in your rearview when the road ahead is in front of you. Stay in your lane!

Make It Happen

Don't rush your process. Trust your process. Keep yourself in a position to learn. When you were a freshman, you waited for your opportunities. The more you learned, and the more you kept yourself ready, the more you earned playing time. When you are seasoned and already know what comes with the game, you start making things happen based on experience and past failures or successes. You know that it won't be easy, but you also know how to approach the game while understanding that no one is going to hand you anything or make excuses or exceptions for you.

I am not here to sell you a dream. I am living proof that if you want something in life, you have to create ways to make it happen. Imagine applying for a job that 1,000 other qualified individuals applied for. You have to separate yourself. 90 percent of these people will apply to a job and wait to get an interview. These are the people that are playing defense. They "kind of" want it. These are the people that will sit and wait on something to come to them that they want. That won't be you after reading this.

There are times when you will have to wait during the application and interviewing process. Not every job or opportunity will be for you.

You just always have to put your best foot forward when you want something. You have to be intentional and aggressive on offense. Do you want the opportunity, or do you want to wait on one like everyone else? If you remain, waiting, in hopes of something, you will be hoping for the rest of your life.

Time Out

When you are on offense and want to score, you will do everything, in your power, to make that happen. If you find ways that it won't, you are playing defense on yourself. Discover how you are blocking yourself and then get on offense and turn your battery all the way up.

Take Action

- Reflect on what it means to be on offense in your life.
- Think of ten ways that you can make something happen that you are in pursuit of.
- What are three defenses or excuses that are stopping you?
- Do you dictate the offense in your life or make excuses about why things won't work?

DEVELOP OTHER SKILLS

"See the Play, Know Your Options"

8

"Don't give up and don't give in, although it seems you never win. You will always pass the test, as long as you keep your head to the sky. You can win, as long as you keep your head to the sky."

-SOUNDS OF BLACKNESS

SONG: OPTIMISTIC

(Sounds of Blackness, 1991)

To be a complete player, you work on your weaknesses but understand and maximize your strengths. Developing other skills doesn't take anything away from your soundness, it only compliments your game. I remember my junior college coach telling me that my game was one dimensional. I took it personally, but she knew my work ethic, day in and day out. Anybody who knew me knows that I wanted to dribble, get to the basket, and score. It worked, but I chose the hard way, instead of shooting a jump shot when necessary.

It wasn't that shooting a jump shot was my weakness, but I had gotten so comfortable relying on my strength of scoring at will that I rarely attempted jump shots. It was too easy to get a bucket at the rim. Shooting a jump shot was not my weakness, I was weak in my confidence in firing a jump shot because I rarely shot them, and it showed. I know that the opposing team scouting report would say, "LET HER SHOOT," because I always willed my way to score at the basket or get fouled to score at the free-throw line.

Remain who you are by sticking with your strengths but be open to being versatile in growing, understanding, and increasing your life opportunities. Life is ever-changing. Those with the flexibility to adapt to changes will not be shocked if they end up in a situation that they need to re-route. If you know that you want to take on a path that puts you in an executive position, for your business or a company, you have to be brave in your approach and confident to be the best that you can be just like you have to in sports.

First, look at the qualities that you already have. In sports, you should have gained many varieties, such as being a team player, developing leadership, understanding time management, and excelling in the discipline. Think of all of the things that you would consider making you a great executive and develop those skills. You have to be the executive in your life. Boss up and be confident in yourself.

You can't just "sort of" know the business or industry that you are in. You can't lack in communication skills because of the position you hold. If you do lack, you can find different ways to develop your communication skills. Communication is all about engaging and listening. Be conscious of your nonverbal habits (body language, eye contact, and posture) and keep people involved so that when they talk, you can listen to understand and respond. When they see you, they know that you are authentic and carry yourself like the boss that you are because you developed those skills with a work ethic to stand where you are.

Invest in Yourself

Investing in yourself is not always monetary. It's about what you can do to thank yourself later. It's about maintaining yourself and being open to other options. Remember to read and see the play. Know that you have options. You are not bound to being robotic. Sometimes you will need to take risks, just make sure they make sense for you.

Continue to educate yourself beyond the school curriculum. Read as often as you can and then be able to form your own opinion based on the perspective you gained and not what someone else stated. There is so much to learn. Don't lose sight of education. It's personally one of my best investments. It's beyond systematic learning. If you want to learn something new, you can read about it, know the facts, and apply the knowledge you acquire.

Don't limit yourself. You will be surprised at how exploring your gifts and having a hobby can turn into other opportunities. Trying as many things that you are interested in, when you can, will keep you outside of the box and your comfort zone. Some of your hobbies could turn into side hustles. If you ever thought about creating content in written or video, photography, designing, cooking, web designing, crafting, blogging, event planning, and even working out as a hobby, then work on these skills. Don't wait for someone to recognize you or to get a particular job. Once again, it is not about the money but putting yourself in the position to develop other skills.

The longer you play sports, the less attention you give to other skills. It is not bad because of your focus on your game, but you should find time when you can, to invest in other skills you would want to use one day. Developing additional skills allows you to gain experience so that you are not starting completely over when it is time for your transition.

Time Out

Do you want to be a complete player or just an average player? When you develop other skills, you keep yourself flexible. There are no limits to what can happen for you when you are flexible. Developing additional skills takes honesty within yourself. Don't have too much pride or ego to ask for help when you want to go to another level. Invest in yourself!

Take Action

- Reflect on other skills that you have developed beyond sports.
- What are three ways that you can invest in developing your personal skills?
- What are two things that you have always wanted to learn?
- What are your most significant investments?

MOVE WITH A PURPOSE
"Be Patient, Use Your Vision, Let the Play Develop"

9

"I'm here to spread a message of hope. Follow your heart. Don't follow what you've been told you're supposed to do."

-J. COLE

(Wash, 2009).

In basketball, our coaches would tell us to be patient, let the play develop, and don't dribble in one spot. When you dribble, it needs to be with a purpose. The ball has to have some direction when you are going to score. Sometimes it is not necessary to dribble, you can do other things within the play if the basketball is not in your hand. That could be setting a teammate up, directing traffic, or communicating with your team. Either way, you were part of the team and put into the game for a reason. You want to make it count. The last thing you want to do is get stagnant and stand in one spot for too long because that will get you sent to the bench with a quickness.

When you make a play in sports, it can be instinctive or natural. When you are patient, at the right time, the vision connects to you, letting the play develop. You might look back when everything is in sync and say, wow. Even if the play is not successful, when you move with a purpose, your attempt displays that the decision was made and influenced by a sense of direction, awareness, and taking risks that put you in a better position.

No one really knows what the future holds, but if you are patient and sit and think about your long-term goals and what you want to do, eventually you will make moves that will progress you in that direction. There is no perfect way or perfect formula. I think that you just have to be aware of what you want your vision to look like. You can be in the same game as another person but see the game in a totally different light.

Don't compare yourself. Comparison withdraws originality. You can find opportunities in every possession if your vision is not limited in a game. Moving with purpose keeps you in the mindset that life does not end with a goal. It's all about a process of continual growth. We don't know what each day, or minute, holds. Having a clear vision and focusing on what's important to you will bridge the gap between your purpose and your passion.

Following what is in your heart to do is what I would consider as moving with a purpose. I can't tell you how to seek your purpose. All

I know is that it brings you peace when you feel that you are right where you are supposed to be and doing what you feel like you should be doing, with peace in your heart. Let it develop, your vision will unfold. It may not look exactly how you imagined it would, but that's the mysterious thing about operating in purpose. My anchor in trusting my faith in God and having a clear focus is what helped me reveal what I'm supposed to be doing right now.

Don't Follow Trends, Follow Your Heart

If you want to be exhausted, go from trend to trend to trend. Eventually, you will experience what it is like to be a trend hopper. You have to do what works for you, what makes you happy, and what gives you a feeling of peace in knowing that you are following your heart.

Be original and do what's in your heart. I was always taught that my life was connected to someone else's blessings. You are not exempt. Your life is a blessing for others. When you follow the trends, though, you blend in with the masses. When you truly follow your heart, you live in a space where you can blossom organically.

If you follow the trends, you will miss out on your original creativity. Find your style and what brings you comfort in your heart.

Trends don't last. Having a passion and following your heart can ignite your legacy. Standing out is more valuable than fitting in. Trying to keep up with trends will not bring you the same happiness of doing what you were created to do.

One of the things you can do is look around you. If you see what everyone else is doing, it will seem like they are competing. When you find your vision to inspire yourself and your journey, you will do the complete opposite. The complete opposite is in following your heart and using the imagination that lives inside of you. You will be moving to your own beat and not try to keep up with the timing of trends. Trends expire. Your life is a marathon that does not expire until you leave. Find your pace and move with a purpose.

Time Out

You may have come across people who tell you what they think is best for you. Let them believe what they want. Find your purpose and operate from a place of peace, knowing that you followed your heart while you were an athlete and when you are transitioning. You are not in a race. Give yourself grace. You are on a journey to become your authentic self and to move with purpose.

Take Action

- Reflect on what the word purpose means to you.
- Have you ever followed a trend, what was the pattern, and how long did it last?
- What does originality look like to you?
- What plays can you set up that will contribute to the vision that you have for your life?

4th Quarter

The End of a New Beginning

CREATE A PLAY

"The Chess Game"

10

"You get to a point where, for whatever reason, the door was just closed, and I had no way to open that door. So I looked the other way, and the door was open, so I walked through."

-BECKY HAMMON

(Wolfe, 2017).

Your coaches equip you with a playbook when you play sports. That playbook is usually broken down, play by play, to what each position can do in each situation to make it ideal for players to score within their system. Your coach may have emphasized that the playbook is only a guideline and advise you not to become robotic within the system. Those guidelines are what help you in your decision making.

Your coach cannot tell you exactly when you will need to use those plays. You study the situation just in case you need to use it. Many factors determine the execution, including the position and timing. The cool thing about a play is that when the game is live, it could be created into another play based on natural development, calculated risks, and instinctive decision making.

In each play, there are options. The options represent what can possibly work. In basketball, one of the most common, free-play situations is the motion offense. This means that any member on the team can create a play and score because all 5 players are in sync, have proper spacing, and do not over-commit to making a specific position score the ball. The players are in constant motion with the ball until someone creates a play out of the movement.

Although you are presented with options within a play, you never know which option will be best until you are in the game situation. Options keep the game flexible and flowing. Plays are simply strategies to implement into a game so that you can be in a position to win. The more you play; you learn that some plays just have to be created and happen naturally.

Whenever I was primarily a point guard on my teams, my coaches would emphasize how important it was for the point guard to know every play, every option, and everyone's position. You are the appointed leader. You have to be trusted to make the best decisions, and this forces you to look at the game in full but play one possession at a time.

To lead, direct, and think for everyone, keeps you ahead of the game and challenges you to see options that could potentially work later. One must trust what they know, verify their trust, get everything centered, and stay on the frontline. When things are going well, and when things are challenging, you have to know when to take a risk and know that life is chess. See how the pieces can work and lead yourself into victory.

TRUST WHAT YOU KNOW, VERIFY THE TRUST, GET EVERYTHING CENTERED, AND STAY ON THE FRONTLINE.

This quote leads me to what I will name the chess game chapter. I learned this quote from one of my vets that I met at a coffee shop one day. His name is Coach John. When we met, I had a few minutes to relax while getting tea and noticed that he was giving a chess lesson. I asked him if I could watch it because I had never played and thought it was hard to learn.

As I sat at the table, drinking my tea, I picked up on how patient his demeanor was. Quickly, I realized that just by listening, I was beginning to learn life lessons through chess by merely being present and listening. After a few minutes, I asked if he could teach me. I started going to take lessons with him. I did want to learn how to play chess, but I was more interested in the life lessons that I gained that I know will benefit you. I will share a few with you:

Control the center. Don't move too quick.

Chess Lesson:

Controlling the center is essential because it allows the other pieces to be flexible. The center is the most crucial area on the chessboard.

Life Lesson:

Knowing what is in your heart and what you are passionate about will come alive when you are centered. The more grounded you are, the more other components in your life will work for you and not against you.

Develop the minor pieces.

Chess Lesson:

Developing the minor pieces will give you an advantage if you prepare them early. This allows you to control the game and avoid any traps that could be set by your opponent.

Life Lesson:

The minor pieces are dominant because they allow the progression of the game to be moved more than one space, at once, when you know each piece's value. Be a student of life. Your minor pieces are other avenues that you can explore. Stay focused on your progression. Don't get trapped.

Don't make moves that help your opponent.

Chess Lesson:

Learn the game and how the pieces work. Your opponent will try to bait you if they see vulnerability in your play.

Life Lesson:

Learn how things operate. Always be confident in your decision making. Remember that you are playing the game, not against someone, not for a position, not to prove a point. Learn what is necessary. Don't be double-minded. Continue to grow and don't revert to old ways or tactics that will hinder you.

Look for moves for development.

<u>Chess Lesson:</u>

When the pieces are developed, they hold more power and increase in value. Don't make pointless exchanges.

<u>Life Lesson:</u>

Work on your personal development. The more you grow, the more valuable you are. Don't waste your time on anything that does not benefit your growth.

You'll find more good moves by accident, not by waiting for an hour.

Chess Lesson:

You want to make the right moves to develop and attack, but you don't want to over calculate. Do not try to memorize patterns and use the same exact formula for each game. Sometimes you have to switch the tactics. Don't be predictable.

Life Lesson:

Taking risks and letting things happen naturally can lead to a great decision. There's no need to over calculate or think too long because you will talk yourself out or doubt the move that you want to make. Make it interesting.

Don't attack because it's in you, only when it works best for you.

Chess Lesson:

Initially, you want to attack to get a checkmate at the first opportunity you see. That will not always work. Once the move is made, you can't take it back.

Life Lesson:

Every opportunity is not a moment to be aggressive. Don't attack just to see if you can win immediately. It's a long game. Attack when it benefits you to push you forward.

Time Out

You have all of the pieces that you need. Until you attempt to create a play, you won't know what the chess pieces can do or how they can benefit you. Chess is a great game to learn and will challenge your thinking. Use the chess pieces that you have, in life, to your advantage.

Take Action

- Reflect on what plays you can create that will advance you to your next level.
- Do you trust in your ability, or do you wait too long and miss out on advancement?
- What are two ways that you can play the cards in your hand?
- Look at all of the pieces around you and find three ways that you can develop each piece.

CONTROL THE FLOW AND TEMPO
"Discipline is Discipline"

11

"Hurry is the greatest enemy of spiritual life in our day. You must ruthlessly eliminate hurry from your life."

-ERNIE JOHNSON

(Homayun, 2017).

As an athlete, one of the first principles that resonate with us is discipline. If we do not follow the guidelines and team rules that our coaches give us, we find ourselves meeting an array of consequences. Discipline is all of the early morning practices, 2-a-days, study hall, and prioritizing life matters when trying to balance life as an athlete and person. It doesn't matter how you look at it, if you are not disciplined in one area of life, you won't be disciplined in another. Discipline is discipline.

Working hard to meet conditioning times and goals in team practices are a sure way to tell if you are learning discipline by taking accountability in yourself and teammates. Remember the consequences your coaches announced about being late to practices or classes? You go out of your way to make sure you all stay accountable. When the whole team suffers, you know that the consequences can range from sprints, bear crawls, and other frowned upon exercises.

Discipline keeps you focused on what you need to do. Distractions are the noises that attempt to knock you down. In your own way, discipline really forces you to grow up early and make beneficial decisions. You know what the consequences are if you have to wake up at 6:00 a.m. but always choose to fall asleep at 1:00 a.m. You will not get the maximum rest or have adequate energy for your day. Your productivity can suffer as a result. That's the consequence of not being disciplined enough to sleep at a reasonable time, giving you a quality night of rest.

That's a small example. The more you set out to do, the more discipline you will need. Lack of control can fester from small areas to other areas in our lives. Be responsible and take ownership of your life. Do everything with excellence, or don't do anything at all. When you are disciplined, you feel good about the results on your journey.

Discipline teaches you how to prioritize what is a priority and what can wait. The value of rewards from your work ethic is a product of discipline. You will quickly realize that there are no short cuts to success. You cannot work on your craft only when you feel like it or devote your effort to foolish things when you have goals. You cannot expect to only take practices to another level if you only go hard the day of or before a game. You have to put in the work every single day and be disciplined in your pursuit.

Find Your Flow

When you find your flow in a game, you find yourself confident in the present and focus on maximizing each moment that you are in. It's almost like you have control of the situation, knowing that everything is aligning. You can feel it, and your purpose is clear. At this point, the flow requires no thinking. Your flow represents trust in your abilities and a focus zone.

What you do not want is to be caught up in a hamster wheel. When you get too comfortable in situations, you will postpone your growth. If you get caught in the wheel, you will not immediately recognize it. You can forget that it is possible to get off of that wheel and stop repeating the same cycles. A hamster doesn't know what it's chasing. That hamster is just running in the same place, with acceleration, and getting winded, only to stop and repeat again. The hamster is going nowhere, extremely fast.

Find your flow in life and know what you are going after. When you move with a purpose and stay poised, patient, and use your vision, the play will develop. Control the tempo. If you do life at one speed, you will either move too fast or move too slow. You have to be able to change your pace and know the seasons of the game. Move at your own pace, you are not in competition with the world.

You give every opportunity your maximum effort in sports and life. Balancing the challenges and skills with discipline will make you unstoppable. This is something that you have to believe for yourself. Have you ever become one with the moment, in a game, and realized that you were in your zone? In the zone, you balance the challenges with your skills.

No moment is too big or too small for you. You are in your zone. You have created a flow that put you in a place of serenity that collided with your passion. Excuse me for getting poetic, but the fact is that you have to be present.

Finding your flow introduces your work ethic, confidence, and focus to the moment that you are in. That moment is free of fear, worry, and distraction. You experience that you are enjoying your process by overcoming challenges and achieving the goals that you set. Lose yourself in purpose and passion. Block out all of the noise along the way. Your flow is your flow. Do not be swayed or jump on someone else's flow because you may find yourself on their hamster wheel. Stay disciplined.

Time Out

There's no need to rush what you want to do or make decisions that don't come from a place of truth. Find your flow and control your tempo. Your race won't be the same pace as the next person. Discipline is discipline, no matter how you look at it. You can't be disciplined in one area of life and not another. Don't be swayed.

Take Action

- Reflect on what finding your flow looks and feels like.
- What pace do you currently feel that you are on?
- What are at least two areas that you can produce better self-discipline?
- What distracts you from staying disciplined?

WINS AND LOSSES

"Don't Forget to Live Your Life."

12

"I decided long ago, never to walk in anyone's shadow,
If I fail, if I succeed, at least I live as I believe,
No matter what they take from me,
They can't take away my dignity"

-WHITNEY HOUSTON

SONG: GREATEST LOVE OF ALL

(Houston, 1985)

Wins and losses are a part of the game. When you win games, it's a great feeling. Everyone is full of joy and looking forward to the next game. Winning shows you that all of the practice and work that you put into the game is paying off. It's the motivating force that tells you that you can overcome obstacles that you had to battle through, one step at a time.

When you lose games, it's not so much of a good feeling. Losses are what teach us and should not bring us down. Sometimes losing brings down the morale of the team and your confidence. Losses are growing pains because they expose the flaws in your game. Suffering should be teaching moments for us, but as human beings, this feeling makes us question ourselves, decisions, and emotions.

Life's wins and losses hit different and really puts you into the perspective that life does go on after sports. Sports will forever be a part of your DNA, a piece of who you are. Either winning or losing, the game should be all about fun. While you want to succeed in everything that you do, it is imperative to understand that learning to lose is a lesson that we must all win. Winning and losing keep us balanced in our lives.

Don't Forget To Live Your Life!

After talking to one of my friends, I realized that not only am I getting older, but I had already lived my childhood dream. I'm forever grateful and honored because, without my journey, you would not be reading this book. Be thankful that you were an anomaly and was fortunate to participate in sports in high school, college, and even the professional level. Everything that sports have taught you has, ironically, prepared you to be as productive in life afterward. Don't look back with regret. Look back with joy.

When I was making my transition from playing, the competitive nature in me always talked about everything that I wanted to accomplish and where I want to be one day. Although you compete with yourself, this feeling will always have you in the mindset of chasing instead of relaxing. Mid conversation, my friend simply said: Don't forget to live your life.

Those words stuck with me. I still have that approach as I take on my life every day. I live for a purpose and to be able to accomplish my life goals. My life goals have nothing to do with a career or business of any sort. Being able to separate and create your own work and life balance is a key to fulfillment.

Don't focus on the word career, focus on positioning yourself for progression in the direction you want your life to go. You have to create the world you want. Live the experience that you have always wanted, no matter how that looks to anyone else. When you breathe and understand that there is never a perfect time to do anything, you will be free of being bound to expectations. It's an everyday battle. Everything that I am telling you is what I try to apply to my life from day-to-day. I am not a perfect human being. I am not here to tell you how to live your life. Just don't forget to live YOUR LIFE.

Welcome new experiences into your world in life and in love. Try not to get overwhelmed with the weight of the world on your shoulders. Don't ask what you can do to leave your legacy on this earth. Just ask yourself what makes you feel alive. In turn, I think your legacy will speak for itself. Be good to people, and please don't forget to be good to yourself.

Sometimes you will be up. Sometimes you will be down. Life is about balance. Money is not the end of the world's problem-solving. The quicker you realize this, the less you will conform to the world around you and focus on your own existence. I'm not an expert, but one thing that I know about money is that it will come and go, along with any other possession in this world. Your life, though, you don't get to choose how long you have, but you can choose the meaning you want your life to have with what you do with your time.

If you ask me, the real dream was already declared as life, liberty, and the pursuit of happiness. Somewhere along the way, we as human beings over fantasized making goldmines in worldly gain and possessions. You could follow the masses and chase the gold mine, but that will leave you in a hamster wheel. I'm not telling you not to make your money. I'm saying you should not make it your only reason for living. Your life is already fabulous!

What they don't tell you about these worldly things we chase is all of the sacrifices we miss out on in life: love, happiness, family, friends, and experiences. The real freedom is already inside of you. Don't get in your own way and create your own chains. You are more than an athlete and more than a job title. Take ownership of your life beyond sports so that when it is your turn to transition, you will be grateful in your journey and see how much more life you have to experience.

Time Out

DON'T FORGET TO LIVE YOUR LIFE!

Take Action

- Reflect on how you want your life to look.
- What is important to you in life?
- What are ten things that you can do to add a different element to your life?
- What brings you peace?

OVERTIME

"Live every single day with purpose. Realize there's no limit to the abundance of potential within you. It's waiting to be awakened by your passion so that you can successfully live your life for an everlasting purpose."

-PERCY MILLER

"MASTER P"

(Miller, 2007)

Now that you have the tools that you can use in your life, I want you to put in the work ethic to really reflect on each principle in the 12 tools that you have gained in your sport and in this written content. Taking ownership of our lives beyond sports is not a one day, one week, or one-year application. We are all on this journey together. This is something that must be applied daily to keep your own life in perspective.

Your purpose is more important than popularity. Having self-awareness and being confident in knowing that your journey was meant to inspire yourself as well as others, is more fulfilling than follow trends. Follow your heart. Always respect yourself, others, and the position you are in. In life, we know that we are not entitled. We work hard and appreciate every opportunity we prepare for. Create your team based on the value that you can give and receive in exchange.

Moving with purpose will allow you to make multiple plays. Don't get stagnant. Find your flow and control the tempo of your life. Wins and losses come with the game. The main objective is to have fun, but in the process, don't forget to live your life. There may be out of bounds guidelines in sports, but there are none in life. Use the boundaries that were created so that you can be creative in your endeavors and growth. Realize that there are no rules, so there should be no excuses in taking ownership of your life beyond sports. You have the tools and the freedom to succeed. It lives inside of you. Believe it!

Bibliography

Coelho, P. (1993). *The Alchemist*. New York: HarperCollins Publishers.

Homayun, O. (2017, May 1). How To Embrace The Unpredictable Moments In Life, With Ernie Johnson, Jr. Retrieved from https://www.forbes.com/sites/omaidhomayun/2017/05/01/how-to-embrace-the-unscripted-moments-with-ernie-johnson jr/#27084b9127c6

Houston, W., (1985). *Greatest Love Of All*. Artista Records, Inc. Songwriters: Michael Masser, Linda Creed

Ibd Staff. (2016, March 15). Quotes Of The Day: Basketball Player Hakeem Olajuwon On Motivation. Retrieved from https://www.investors.com/news/management/wisdom-to-live-by/quotes-of-the-day-basketball-player-hakeem-olajuwon-on-motivation/

Miller, P., (2007). *Guaranteed Success When You Never Give Up By Percy Miller*.

Mitchell, J. (2018, March 1). The Art Of Being Self-Made: A Conversation With Nipsey Hussle. Retrieved from

https://www.forbes.com/sites/julianmitchell/2018/03/01/the-art-of-being-self-made-a-conversation-with-nipsey-hussle/

Mufasa, (2019). *The Lion King Movie*.

Sounds of Blackness. (1991). *Optimistic*. A&M Records. Producers: Gary Hines, Jimmy Jam, Terry Lewis

Thomas, E., 2011. *The Secret To Success*. Goldsboro, N.C.: Spirit Reign Pub.

Vaynerchuk, G., & Vaynerchuk, G. (2016, April 14). Nonprofit Marketing: The Same Rules Apply. Retrieved from https://www.garyvaynerchuk.com/nonprofitmarketing-the-same-rules-apply/

Walker, H. M. (2015, May 15). My Sporting Life, Without The Sports. Retrieved from https://www.huffpost.com/entry/my-sporting-life-without-_b_6858846

Wash, S. (2009, September 19). Jay-Z Protege J. Cole Takes Unusual Path to Stardom. Retrieved from https://abcnews.go.com/Entertainment/cole-jay-zs-protege-attended- college-closer-idol/story?id=8605048

Wolfe, A. (2017, April 28). Becky Hammon's Big Shot. Retrieved from https://www.wsj.com/amp/articles/becky-hammons-big-shot-1493393914

Acknowledgments

First, I would like to thank God for being my anchor and giving me the vision of completing this book and the acronym for T.O.O.L's to mean Taking Ownership of Our Lives Beyond Sports. This literally came to me as I looked around and saw that there were not many platforms or people discussing it. Being a former athlete, I was almost caught in the cycle of losing my whole identity inside of sports and could not see past wanting to play. This can be toxic and hinder us from fulfilling the experiences and purpose we are supposed to be doing in life.

My family and friends. Your role in this project could not have been more inspiring. My best friends for really understanding my vision and keeping me inspired. My sister, for being the first to read a page from the manuscript. I'm so grateful to each and every one of you! There are so many people to name, but I promise nothing has ever gone unnoticed.

My first mentor, Coach Thompson. Thank you for investing in me and genuinely opening my mind to learning more about life than basketball. I really appreciate you for believing in me and not giving me answers or suggestions that I had many questions about. Instead, you annoyed me by telling me to look it up and figure it out.

Next, thank you to Onney with Onney Publishing. I would have never known that one interaction, a decade ago, would turn into you truly believing in me and giving me the one-on-one consultation that was so needed to put me in 5th gear in this project. Thank you for seeing my vision and always being in my corner.

Coach Taylor, my junior college coach. You showed me the true definition of what family is away from home and what I was used to. You challenged me to become a better person and to see what I had in front of me, to truly maximize the present.

About the Author

(Photo 2019 WISE/R Symposium: Complimentary Headshot)

PATRINA GOREE is a former high school, collegiate, and professional basketball player from Houston, Texas. She found purpose in T.O.O.L's Beyond Sports as a way to tell her story while reaching the sports community. Goree graduated from Jack Yates High School in 2010 and received her Master of Arts in Strategic Communication from Liberty University. Goree wrote her first book in 2016, Evolving Conscious & Pulse Power, which is a book of poetry. In 2020 she started a business, (PDG Family Holdings, LLC), assisting businesses with strategic planning & consulting, along with other services.

www.ingramcontent.com/pod-product-compliance
Lightning Source LLC
Chambersburg PA
CBHW060837170426
43192CB00019BA/2804